Bob + Pam

All the Best!

Tom Klobucher

TALES *of* GRATITUDE

A SHORT STORY BOOK

TALES *of* GRATITUDE

Stories to Inspire Thankfulness

TOM KLOBUCHER

This book is lovingly dedicated to my parents,
John and Rose Ann Klobucher.

Despite the many hardships that they experienced,
they always maintained a profoundly grateful attitude
about life in America.

Table of Contents

Acknowledgments .... *ix*

Read This First: Why I Wrote This Book—
and What I Hope You Gain from It .... *xi*

STORY #1: "Information Please" 1

STORY #2: "The Saturday Clothes" 9

STORY #3: "The Paper Route" 19

STORY #4: "The Tallest Little Christmas Tree" 31

STORY #5: "The Tall View" 43

STORY #6: "Take My Hand" 51

STORY #7: "The Copper Mine" 67

STORY #8: "The Dream of America" 77

STORY #9: "The Printer's Devil" 87

STORY #10: "Cinderella and the Plugger" 101

STORY #11: "Helen's Story" 115

STORY #12: "The Tailor's Magic Coat" 125

STORY #13: "The Dukes of the Rails" 137

AFTERWORD: Taking Stock 155

Epilogue *159*

Acknowledgments

First and always, I want to give thanks to God the Father, who offers to us all the Fatherhood of God—the opportunity to be adopted into his forever family, if we will put our faith and trust in Him alone.

My deep gratitude goes out to my father and mother, John and Rose Klobucher; my wife Carol, who is my soul mate, my partner, my best friend and encourager, and the one person who always makes me want to be a better man; and my two children, Lisa and Paul, their spouses, Mark and Amy, and their five children, Kate, Jenna, Seth, Caden and Kelsy.

I am especially grateful to God for the memory of my oldest sister, Rose K. Kammerling, who saved my life and guided me as a young man to do the right thing, and who was always there for me in times of need. She was a solid rock of strength.

Thanks go out to all of the associates at our firm, Thomas Interiors, who make it a truly Great Place to Work.

And I also want to thank Mike Cleary, my editor and friend, who guided and inspired me to stay the course on this, my seventh book; Stuart Hackett, my very competent assistant on this project, who helped me to stay on track and brought significant input and wisdom in numerous areas of the book; Jerry Dorris of AuthorSupport.com for the cover design and layout of the book interior, along with much advice along the way; my longtime friend Ed Hoover, who was the first person to tell me I needed to write books, and Ray Pritchard, mentor and friend, Lee Streater, Archie Parrish, Dan Sullivan, Martha Akre, Dann Spader, and all the others who offered support, advice and encouragement along the way.

Special thanks go to you, the reader for investing your time and attention in this book. My hope is that you will be blessed by it, and that you will share it with others who have not yet found the joy of a fully engaged life of gratitude.

Read This First

WHY I WROTE THIS BOOK—
AND WHAT I HOPE YOU GAIN FROM IT

I have called the stories in this book tales of gratitude because each one carries a life lesson for which I am deeply grateful. I believe each lesson has the capacity to change someone's life dramatically, quickly, and for the better.

Each of the narratives you will find here is built around something important I learned along the way, something that ended up making a big difference, not only to me, but to the people who matter most to me. It may seem old-fashioned to suggest that reading a book like this should deliver more than entertainment or the satisfaction of intellectual curiosity—that a story should carry a clear lesson, a takeaway, something that everybody who hears it can understand in the same way, implement, and benefit from. Maybe it is old-fashioned. In that case, I'm willing to take the risk of doing things the old-fashioned way.

When I was very young, my father used to share stories with

me at the end of his workday. He never wrote these stories down. He always spoke from his heart. As he smoked his pipe, he would reminisce about his early life in Yugoslavia, about his passage to America, and about the struggles, setbacks, and joys he experienced in his adopted country. When he told these stories, he seemed to open up entire new worlds for both of us. I would listen with all the rapt attention of youth, watching the smoke swirl above his head like the twists of fate themselves. I was eager to take in every detail my father chose to share with me. I noticed that he was fond of ending a story with a clear moral, closing his tale by reminding me about the importance of standing behind the quality of your work, or the necessity of perseverance in the face of adversity, or the reality that family is, at the end of the day, what matters most.

I believe that lessons like these are not only worth putting into print, but also worth sharing together, as a family. That has been my aim here: To bring important lessons to life through stories that people will be inspired, not just to experience silently, but to read aloud to their loved ones.

My hope is that the tales I've included in this collection will help you to build bridges between you and the people who matter most to you, the way my father's stories built a bridge between him and me. My hope is that these stories will open up new possibilities and fresh beginnings for everyone who comes in contact with them. My hope is that you and those you love will be transformed by the power of story, as I was transformed. That is a lot to hope for, perhaps—but one of the lessons my father shared with me when I was a boy was to aim high, and I see no reason to stop following that advice now.

INFORMATION PLEASE

"Family need not be defined merely as those with whom we share blood."

—CHARLES DICKENS

A few days ago, I was passing the nut display outside our local grocery store, when I developed an unusual and almost insatiable desire to buy a bag of walnuts. I don't know why this happened. I hadn't eaten walnuts in years, but as I

1

looked at them, attractively arranged in a wicker basket between the chestnuts and peanuts, I got a strong sense that something delectable lay beneath that hard grey armor.

I bought a small bag of them and took it home. Then I ran into a problem. Our nutcracker was broken. I went to the toolbox to get a hammer, but the toolbox wasn't there. I remembered lending it to a neighbor, who had yet to return it.

The walnuts lay still in their bag on the kitchen counter. I knew they would taste perfect, if I could just get them open.

"How," I wondered out loud, "does one crack a walnut shell without a nutcracker or a hammer?"

As soon as I had spoken, my cell phone, which was on the counter beside the walnuts, gave a familiar trill and spoke. (It was one of those so-called "smart" phones.)

"Walnuts," said a voice from the phone, "can be opened using a knife. Use the blade of the knife to pry the two halves of the shell apart."

Surprised, I picked up the phone and saw that detailed instructions had appeared on the screen, along with a diagram.

This episode reminded me of a story I had heard from a friend, Jane Bennington, some time before. Jane had been complaining that despite the amazing technology that powered them and the opportunities they now provided, phones had lost something important. She remembered the days when you had to pick up a phone and speak to another person—an operator—before making your call.

"It was more human then," said Jane.

Jane told me a story she had heard years ago about a little boy called Toby who lived in the Pacific Northwest.

When Toby was very young, his family became one of the first in their neighborhood to have a phone. Toby was fascinated by the phone from the outset. He would watch in fascination as his mother used it to call his father, who worked a long distance away and was rarely home.

One day, Toby was playing in the backyard when he fell off the swing and bumped his head. Nobody was home, his mother having left a few minutes earlier to buy milk at the local store. Toby went into the house, clutching his sore head. Not knowing whom to talk to, he picked up the phone in the hall and said, in a tearful voice, "Information please."

Unexpectedly, a voice responded, "Information."

"I bumped my head," Toby said.

"Oh dear," said the woman's voice on the other end of the line. "How did you do that?"

"I fell off the swing," he answered, sobbing.

"And where is your mom?"

"She's gone to the store."

"Will she be back soon?"

"Yes."

"Is there any blood?" said the voice.

Toby put his hand on the back of his head and felt the swollen lump rising beneath his hair. He brought his fingers back in front of his face and examined them. "No," he said, "just a big bump."

"That's okay," said the woman's voice. "Just get a big piece of ice from the refrigerator and hold it against the bump. That will stop it hurting and make the swelling go down."

After that, Toby picked up the phone and called his friend "Information Please" whenever he needed help. He called her when he couldn't answer all the questions in his math homework, and she went through the nine times table with him. He called her when he found a baby hedgehog in the garden, and she told him to feed it bread in a bowl of warmed up milk. He called her when he was writing an English assignment. "How do you spell jewelry?" he asked, and she patiently recited the letters to him. He called her when he had an argument with his sister, and she said, "Brothers and sisters argue, Toby, and that's okay. But it's important to listen to what your sister says and try to show her that you understand how she feels."

One sad morning, Toby came downstairs to discover his pet canary, Pepe, lying limp and lifeless on the floor of his cage. He called Information Please.

4

"Why," he asked, "could something that sings such beautiful songs wind up all cold and dead?"

"There are other worlds to sing in, Toby," she said.

Not long after this, Toby's family moved across the country to New Hampshire, where there was a different phone system and a different operator. He greatly missed Information Please. She had been his friend, and as he grew up, he always remembered her.

Some years later—twelve years after his last call with Information Please—Toby traveled to his boyhood hometown of Portland for a business meeting. He stopped by a pay phone to make a few calls, and without really thinking about what he was doing, dialed the operator and said, "Information please."

Amazingly, the voice that responded was the same voice he had known so well in his youth. "Information," his old friend said nonchalantly, not yet having recognized his voice.

"How do you spell jewelry?" asked Toby.

For several moments, the line was completely silent.

Then the familiar voice spoke again.

"I hope your head is feeling better."

Toby laughed. He talked with Information Please for some time. She told him that her name was Alice. He told her how much he had missed their talks after he moved away.

"I don't know if you realize how much I've missed them too," said Alice. "I had no children. Your calls meant a great deal to me."

Before they ended the call, Toby agreed to call Alice again the next time he was in the area.

A few months later, Toby had to visit Portland again. Once again, he dialed the operator.

This time, a different voice said, "Information."

"I was hoping to talk to Alice," said Toby.

There was a pause.

"Who is calling, please?" said the unfamiliar voice.

"It's Toby, an old friend."

"Well, Toby," she said, "I am so sorry to have to tell you this, but Alice died two months ago. She had been ill for some time."

Toby was about to end the call, when the operator said, "Wait, did you say your name was Toby?"

"Yes."

"Then Alice left a message for you. She said to read it to you if you called. It says, 'Toby, there are other worlds to sing in.'"

For a few moments, Toby could not speak.

"Do you know what that means?" said the operator.

"Yes," he said.

Looking down at my cell phone and the uncracked walnut in my hand, I knew too. Toby's calls to Alice had a big impact on both of their lives. My friend Jane was right about human

6

contact. Even the smallest of actions can make a big difference to other people. This is one of life's miracles. This is gratitude!

"Friends are the family you choose."

—JESS C. SCOTT

THE SATURDAY CLOTHES

"Youth cannot know how age thinks and feels. But the old are guilty if they forget what it was to be young."

—J.K. ROWLING

When Eileen was four years old, she had a morning ritual. She used to wake up early and wait outside her parents' bedroom to see what color shirt her father would be wearing when he emerged.

Eileen's father, Bill, was a businessman. He was a very busy man. Bill had a company to run, and he always dressed in a suit and tie on days when he had to go to the office. The shirt he wore with his suit and tie was always white. Eileen still had a little trouble with the days of the week—she wasn't always sure which day came after Tuesday—but she knew one thing with absolute certainty about the way the week unfolded, and that was that her dad never, ever wore a colorful shirt to work. She knew that whenever he emerged from his bedroom wearing a colorful shirt, it was going to be Saturday that day. Saturday was her favorite day. Saturday was the day Eileen got to spend time with her dad.

One morning, as he went downstairs for his morning coffee, Bill spotted Eileen waiting in the hall and noticed that she looked sad.

"What's the matter, princess?" he asked.

"It's your shirt, Daddy."

"My shirt? What's wrong with it?"

"It's white. I like it better when you wear a shirt with colors on it. That makes it Saturday."

Bill smiled, kneeled down, and looked straight into his daughter's eyes so he could be sure that she would know he was listening very closely.

"Is that what makes it Saturday?" he asked. "The kind of shirt I wear?"

"Yes," Eileen said. She still looked a bit sad, but the fact that her dad was now eye to eye with her and smiling at her made the beginnings of a smile appear at one corner of her mouth.

"And do you like Saturdays better than other days?" her dad continued.

Eileen nodded.

"Why is that, sweetheart?"

Eileen sniffed, rubbed her nose, and said, "When it's Saturday and you have a colored shirt on, you and I get to do things. You don't have to go to the office. Saturday is the best day of all."

Bill nodded, smiled, and said, "It is, Eileen. I know it is. Saturday is the very best day. Can you guess what day it is today?"

Eileen shook her head no.

"Today," her dad said, "is Friday. That means the best day of our whole week, Saturday, happens tomorrow. We only have one more day to wait."

Now a big, bright smile spread across Eileen's little face.

"And I have an idea," her dad continued. "Do you want to hear what it is?"

Eileen nodded.

"I think you and I should pick out a special colored shirt for me to wear every Saturday—and only on Saturday—so that we know it's our special time. Does that sound like fun? We could do that right now, before I go to work."

Eileen nodded again, and her dad made a "shh" sound and put his fingers to his lips.

"Mommy's still asleep," he said, "so be very, very quiet, okay?"

Eileen nodded wordlessly, and her dad grinned and led her into the master bedroom, where Eileen's mother was indeed fast asleep, sighing softly on the big bed. Eileen's dad opened the closet where he kept all his shirts, pressed and hung up neatly.

"Take a look," he whispered, gesturing to the closet. "Which one will be the Saturday shirt?"

Eileen scanned the contents of the closet. On one side, hanging from a rack, were a couple of clean, pressed, white dress shirts, the kind that said: "Daddy's about to go to work." On the other side of the rack were many colorful, exciting, adventurous shirts, shirts that said: "Daddy's about to spend time with Eileen." She took a long time inspecting the shirts on that side of the closet, until finally one caught her eye that seemed special. It was a light blue denim snap shirt. For some reason it reminded her of Christmas. She ran her little hand across it. It was all soft and inviting and relaxed, the way Saturdays were with her dad. It was the opposite of a crisp, pressed work shirt.

"That one," she said.

Her dad smiled. "Okay," he whispered. "That's our Saturday shirt."

*   *   *   *   *

The next day, Eileen watched her dad pull the blue denim shirt off the hanger, put it on, and quickly snap it in place. He turned to face his daughter in the doorway. With a big smile on his face he said, "Happy Saturday!" With that, Eileen ran into her dad's arms and gave him a huge hug and kiss.

With a chuckle, Bill said, "What do you wish to do today, my princess?"

Beaming, Eileen said, "I just want to be with you all day, Daddy. As long as you are with me, and as long as it's Saturday, I don't care what we do!"

Their first stop was the carwash, a fascinating place to watch Dad's dirty, driverless car go through the automated car wash, only to exit clean as a whistle. Then three or four attendants surrounded the car with towels in hand to wipe it dry. What a thrill to watch!

Next on the agenda was the local doughnut shop, where the doughnuts were always fresh out of the oven. It smelled like heaven. The doughnuts came in every flavor and color you could imagine, and they were served with the best hot chocolate and the coffee Dad loved.

After the doughnut shop, they visited the local park to watch people play soccer and baseball. At the park you could always see lots of people jogging on the trails or walking with their puppies. Eileen ran around for a bit, but once the swings caught her attention, she sprinted over to them. Transfixed on the swings, Eileen yelled, "Daddy! Daddy! Come push me!" She loved it when her strong dad propelled her forward on the swings, and Bill always cherished his daughter's shouts of joy.

After some time at the park, Eileen was starting to tire out. They got back into the car and headed to the cleaners to pick up a new batch of crisp, clean shirts for the coming work week. Eileen wasn't crazy about this stop, because it signaled that Saturday was closer to being over than she wanted to admit, but she knew that this leg of the journey also meant a trip to the candy bowl the owner of the shop kept on the counter.

Once Bill's shirts were picked up, they headed to the gas station. This was always one of Eileen's favorite stops because her dad would let her help him pump the gas. She hopped proudly out of the car and marched right over to the pump. With her father's large hands gently guiding her, she put her little hands on the gas pump and pulled the handle. She always felt so grown up when she heard the snap of the pump letting her know the tank was full.

Next, it was time to head back home to help Daddy cut the

grass. The yard was small, but it was full of lush, green grass. The lawnmower was a push mower, the type with no motor. Eileen loved to help mow the thick grass, because her dad helped her. If you had happened to see them pushing the mower that day, you would have seen a huge smile on each of their faces.

Next was story time. Bill loved to tell stories about himself when he was a little boy, and Eileen loved to listen to them. Then came lunch. Mom served up Eileen's favorite and called it "The "Saturday Special"—tomato soup and French bread. Eileen relished it. After she had finished lunch with Mommy and Daddy, she knew it was time for a nap. Of course, there was always another story first.

As Eileen's dad tucked her in for her afternoon nap, she played with the pocket of his Saturday shirt, unsnapping and snapping the clasp on the pocket, secretly hoping there would be a surprise for her in there. In fact, there was: A lemon gumdrop, just for her. Eileen smiled and tucked it away under her pillow. Her eyelids were getting heavy now, and she drifted off to sleep with the image of her dad in his Saturday shirt closing the door to her room.

* * * * *

Thirty-five years later, Eileen was late. She was at least twenty minutes behind schedule in getting ready for work. She'd overslept—again. It was going to be a full day. There were project updates to review...a big problem in Shipping that had something to do with a software update that had gone wrong...a meeting with Sales at 2:00 that she was not looking forward to, given how far behind quota most of the team members were, and...

"Mommy?"

Eileen, who had been headed downstairs to grab a much-needed cup of coffee and wolf down the breakfast she knew her husband had prepared for her, stopped in midstride. The voice belonged to Tommy—her four-year-old son—and it sounded vaguely sad.

She turned and looked at him—and something about the expression on his face matched the tone of his voice and made her heart wobble a little.

"Yes, honey. What is it?"

"Can you go back in your room and change into another dress? Please?"

There was a brief silence in the hallway as Eileen considered these words. She took a deep breath, walked slowly to her son, kneeled down so she could look straight into his eyes, and said:

"Why do you want me to do that, honey?"

"Because when you wear clothes like the ones you have on now, you go away, and you don't come back until late, late at night. Please put on some different clothes, Mommy."

Eileen took another deep breath and thought long and hard about how best to respond to her son's request. She had certainly been working long hours, and they must have been taking a toll on Tommy. She closed her eyes to try to keep the tears from flowing, but they trickled down her face anyway. She kept her eyes shut for a long moment, and as she did so, she saw, for the briefest instant, a blue denim shirt hanging in a long-forgotten closet, waiting for the chance to bring Saturday to life again.

"Tommy, can I ask you something?"

The little boy nodded.

"Do you know what day it is today?"

He slowly shook his head no.

Eileen smiled. "It's Friday," she said. "And that means we have only one more day to go before Saturday. And on Saturday, no matter what else happens, I get to spend the whole day with you. Saturday is special. In fact, there's something very special about it that I forgot to tell you and Daddy. Can I tell you what it is right now?"

Curious now, Tommy nodded again.

"When I was a little girl, my daddy used to have a special shirt that he only wore on Saturday. A blue denim shirt with snaps. He wore it just for me. And whenever I saw him wearing that shirt, I knew it was going to be our day together. Would you like to help me pick out something like that to wear—something that's just

17

for our special day together? If you help me pick it now, I could wear it tomorrow. We can call it my 'Saturday clothes.'"

Tommy was smiling now. "How long will you wear your Saturday clothes?" he asked.

"All day long, sweetie," she said, "from the time I get up until the time you go to bed. And as long as I'm wearing my Saturday clothes, that's our time."

They went in, hand in hand, and started looking through her closet. She was still late for work, of course, but that didn't seem to matter as much now. She had found her Saturday clothes. And she knew she would keep her promise. That's gratitude!

"The way we interact with our children becomes their inner voice."

—PEGGY O'MARA

THE
PAPER ROUTE

*"Pray as though everything depends on God—and
work as though everything depends on you."*

—ST. AUGUSTINE

When I was ten years old and convinced for some reason
that I had reached the point in life where I knew everything I needed to know, I decided I had a right to earn some
more pocket money. This was late September of 1971.

I don't remember exactly what it was that I wanted to buy. It might have been comic books, or gum, or movie tickets. I suppose it doesn't really matter what I planned to use the money for. What matters now is what I recall most vividly about the decision—that my buddies all seemed to have plenty of ready cash for these kinds of purchases, and I didn't. That wasn't fair. The unfairness made my stomach growl and made me vow to catch up, somehow, with the guys who had far, far better dads than I did. My dad was a cheapskate.

I knew better than to ask my own dad for an increase in my allowance. That request had gotten shot down the last four times I'd made it. There had to be another way to expand my budget. I just hadn't found it—yet.

Someone in my circle of friends at school mentioned during recess that they were looking for boys to deliver the evening paper in our city. I saw my opportunity.

That night, over dinner, I said to my father, "I think I ought to start delivering the evening paper like some of my friends do. It pays five dollars a week. That would keep me from having to ask you all the time for more allowance money. I know how irksome it is when I bother you with that kind of thing, Dad." I was proud of that word, "irksome," having recently mastered it in preparing for a spelling bee at school. Surely he would be impressed with that.

My mom smiled quietly, but my dad only stared down at his lamb stew with a scowl on his face. He wasn't impressed at all. He was going to say no.

My stomach twisted again. Why in the world had I gotten my hopes up? I had to have the meanest dad in the whole city. All my friends got to buy comic books and go to movies and chew gum whenever they wanted to. But I was stuck with a half-dollar a week. It wasn't fair!

I heard a little bumping sound from under the table. In the years since, I've come to wonder whether it might have been my mom giving my dad a gentle kick in the shins, but at the time I had no such inkling. All I knew was that my dad grimaced a little bit right after the little bumping sound, and that the scowl turned into a neutral—almost thoughtful—gaze into his bowl.

My mom asked, in a casual tone: "What do you think, Harold?"

"We'll see," he replied.

* * * * *

The next night, over dinner—to my astonishment—my dad brought the subject up.

"About that paper route..." he said, shaking parmesan cheese onto his spaghetti and meatballs. "Your mother and I had a talk."

Mom said nothing. Now it was her turn to stare down at her dinner.

21

My dad, though, shifted his gaze as he put the parmesan cheese down on the table. Now he was staring straight at me.

"Billy," he said, "I told your mother I thought it was a terrible idea, and I'll tell you why I said that. First and foremost, you're only ten years old. That's not old enough to do a job like this. Most of the boys who have paper routes are at least twelve—I checked. Second, delivering a paper is likely to have a bad effect on your grades. Your grades are excellent, and I want them to stay that way. Third, this is a big city, and strange things can happen to a boy who's out riding around the streets on his own. You just haven't thought this through. I don't want anything to happen to you, Billy. Those are the reasons I gave your mother for turning down your request to take on a paper route. And I think they're good reasons."

My stomach was doing backflips again. Just as I had suspected: I really did have the meanest dad in the entire city. Maybe the entire state.

There was a long and uneasy silence at the table. Nobody ate anything. My dad kept staring at me like I'd stolen something.

"However," my dad said, "your mother had a different opinion."

My mom looked up and gave me a gentle smile. All of a sudden my stomach felt better and the dining room was a little brighter.

"Your mother is of the opinion that this could be a good learning experience for you—that we should encourage you to be more self-sufficient, and that delivering papers every day is a perfect opportunity for doing just that. So based on her advice, I'm willing to consider letting you take on this paper route—on one condition."

"What's the condition?" I asked, breathless. I was certain he was about to set the bar impossibly high by telling me that I had to put half the money I earned in the church collection plate every Sunday and save the rest for college or something.

"If you do this—and again, I think it's a bad idea—but if you do this, you have to promise us that you'll keep the paper route for at least a year. No quitting. That's the condition. Your mother and I are in full agreement about that, by the way."

A miracle! That was easy! Probably Mom's idea, come to think of it! Why *wouldn't* I want extra pocket money for a whole year?

My mom asked: "So, is it a deal, Billy?" She was looking at me, and I could tell she was trying not to smile.

"It's a deal," I said. And I meant it.

* * * * *

Delivering papers started out for me as the most enjoyable chore I'd ever had. It wasn't really a chore, actually—not like taking out the garbage or washing the dishes after dinner. It was fun. This was *my* job. I got to listen to the radio as I folded up and rubber-banded all the day's papers in the garage after school. And I got to ride my bike around the neighborhood with a cool canvas satchel slung over my shoulder. Best of all, I was earning my own money now, and everyone in the neighborhood knew it.

I loved my job—in September and early October, that is. Come mid-October, though, I realized that there were certain factors I hadn't taken into account. The first of these was a driving rainstorm that refused to let up.

"Don't even think about skipping your route today," my dad said. "You made a deal. No quitting. You've got some papers to fold, I think. Get to work."

He had seen me staring out the window with a melancholy gaze at those big sheets of rain that were coming down.

I didn't say anything out loud, but inside, I thought, *Why couldn't I skip one day and just deliver two papers tomorrow?*

But I didn't skip the route. I knew I had made a deal, and I knew I had to stick to it. I folded up the papers, put rubber bands around them, tossed them into plastic bags, gathered them into my satchel, threw on a poncho, opened the garage door, and headed outside on my bike. As I delivered my papers that day, I thought I noticed a pair of headlights far behind me—they seemed to stay three or four blocks away. I wondered if maybe I was being followed, but I decided I was just imagining things. All that afternoon, as the cold rain drenched my face, I replayed the story I was telling myself about what had happened to me:

My dad was making me keep a promise that any other dad would have let his son break.

When I got back, drenched and exhausted, my mom started making me some tomato soup to warm me up. But my dad said, "You left the garage door open, Billy. Go close it before you sit down to eat." A lot he cared if I caught pneumonia! As I shut the garage door, I noticed the car was making those funny clicking, cooling-down noises a car makes when someone has just driven it. I thought to myself, *My dad must have gone out on a pleasure cruise, while his son was pedaling and shivering in the worst rainstorm of the year.*

I began to wonder whether the extra pocket money I enjoyed each week was worth the effort.

And come November, it began to seem like I had made an even worse deal than I'd imagined. A bitter cold snap set in—the worst in twenty years, the radio said. The thermometer on the porch read five degrees. Was I really supposed to deliver papers in such weather? Apparently I was. My dad said, "A deal is a deal, Billy. Bundle up, fold your papers, and hit the road. Wear a scarf. Wear your mittens. The sooner you get the papers delivered, the sooner you'll be back home where it's warm. Get moving." My mom coughed a little cough from the kitchen, but if this was supposed to be some kind of signal for my dad to ease up, he missed it. The route was freezing—actually, it was well below freezing, come to think of it—and every once in a while I'd catch sight of what looked like those same distant headlights behind me. But who would be silly enough to want to follow me around? The bitter cold, along with what my dad had said about strange things happening in the city, must have had me imagining things.

When I got back, our car was doing that same cooling-off, tick-tick-tick thing in the garage. I knew exactly what that meant. My dad had been out driving around for the fun of it, taking it easy behind the wheel, probably with the heat going full blast, while I was out freezing and pedaling and tossing papers onto frigid porches!

When December rolled around, I became convinced that the five bucks a week was peanuts compared to what I was going through. Not only was it getting dark earlier and earlier—I hadn't planned on delivering my papers at night!—there was the problem of blizzards. Snow squalls definitely *weren't* part of my plan when I agreed to do this paper route for a whole year. But there was Old Man Winter, lashing our neighborhood with at least a foot of the white stuff. Did my dad expect me to get out in the middle of this weather and complete my route?

He certainly did. "You've got a job to do, Billy," he said as he saw me staring out the window at the accumulating snow drifts. "You took it on. You promised not to quit. So you'd better get out and do it." My mom gave him a stern look from the hallway, but he didn't seem to pay her any mind.

The streets had been plowed, which made pedaling my bike possible. Not exactly easy, but possible. Along about the third block on my route, though, disaster struck. My bike's chain snapped. There was now no way to get anywhere using that beloved old two-wheeler of mine.

I knew I couldn't go back to the house with my satchel full of papers. My dad wouldn't stand for that. So I did the only two things I could think of. I settled my satchel into place, and I began walking my paper route.

On a functioning bike, the route usually only took me about thirty minutes. But now I found myself *walking* the route, in heavy falling snow, pulling along the useless bike by my side, with most of the houses on my list still to go. The snow fell still and silent around me, and seemed to say what I imagined my dad saying: "Get moving. Don't quit. Get moving. Don't quit. Get moving. Don't quit."

Several minutes later, a bright light cast shadows onto the snow ahead of me. It was at that moment that I turned and noticed the headlights slowly approaching from behind me.

My stomach clenched with anxiety. My unpleasant evening was about to get worse. Hadn't my father warned me about crazy things happening to kids who wandered all on their own around the big city? Hadn't he told me I was too young for this job?

The lights drew closer. I started to shiver. Something bad was about to happen. I knew it.

But then, I noticed something that surprised me. My stomach unclenched, and I drew in a big breath of relief and smiled. This wasn't some random person who'd been following me as I delivered my papers. This was our car. This was my dad.

The car pulled over to the side of the snowy road, and my dad got out. The sound of the door shutting was solid and familiar. He walked toward me, strong and purposeful.

"Trouble with your bike, Son?" he said.

I nodded. I had never been so glad to see him. It took me a moment to get the words out. "Chain gave out," I said, and I gestured toward the crippled bicycle that lay in the snow, where I had let go of it several seconds before.

"Let's get it into the car," he said. Together, we maneuvered it into the back seat, mangled chain and all. It was a tight fit. The door just closed.

"Get in, Son," my dad said gently. "We'll finish this route together tonight."

* * * * *

As we drove home, my route complete for the night, I turned to

28

face my dad. His eyes were on the road and his hand was steady on the wheel. The snow fell on the windshield, and the wipers pushed the snow away in a calm, predictable rhythm. The car was warm.

"Maybe you were right, Dad," I said. "Maybe I am too young for a job like this."

He looked over at me and smiled, then trained his gaze back on the road.

"I don't know about that," he said. "You've done all right. I think you'll be fine."

I smiled and settled back into my seat and watched the road, just like he was watching it.

"Dad?"

"Yes?"

"Did you get in trouble for closing up shop early to drive behind me whenever the weather was bad?"

"Oh no, Son. Mr. Miller understood. He has a boy, too. About your age. Nobody's in any trouble."

"Dad?"

"Yes?"

"Thank you for doing that."

"Well, I had to, didn't I, Billy?"

"You did?"

"Sure I did."

"Why's that?"

"Well, Billy," my dad said, "the moment you promised not to quit, I did, too."

The years have passed, like they do, and countless rainstorms and cold snaps and blizzards have passed with them, but the ride back home that night has stayed with me, and always will stay with me, as long as I have memories to cherish. That ride back home was when I realized I had the very best dad in the world. I was so grateful for that, and I still am.

"Behind every young child who believes in himself is a parent who believed first."

—Matthew Jacobson

THE TALLEST
LITTLE
CHRISTMAS TREE

*"God seeks to influence humanity. This is at the heart
of the Christmas story. It is the story of light coming
into the darkness, of a Savior to show us the way of light
overcoming the darkness, of God's work to save the world."*

—ADAM HAMILTON

In the late summer of 1927, Carl Crawdie, who was eight years old, contracted polio after a swimming party at Taggart's

Pond. He was the only one affected. For some time, just about everybody in Grindleaf, West Virginia thought he was going to die. The week after the virus attacked his body, solemn faces crowded around his bed, and the curtains were kept closed.

Carl hated the curtains being closed. For one thing, it made everything dark and gloomy. For another, it meant that he couldn't see the finches that nested in the eave just above his window. They were training their young to fly, and the window sill made a perfect launch pad. He could hear them chattering even when the curtains were closed, rustling about outside the glass.

An outdoor boy and a climber of countless trees before polio claimed him, he had always loved animals and enjoyed a special connection with them. If anyone else had opened the window beside the finches' nest, they would have flitted away in an instant. When Carl came near, the finches went on about their business just as if he were one of them. He felt like he was one of them, in a way, except that he couldn't fly.

He survived the polio, but even when he got better, he found that he couldn't use one of his legs at all. The muscles had become withered. Carl's dad couldn't stand to see the way the leg weighed him down, so he carved him a crutch out of the branch of an oak tree. The wood pressed against Carl's armpit, though, causing painful blisters. He didn't like the crutch.

Another consequence of Carl being ill was that his family

seemed to be even poorer than before. There had been doctor's fees, of course—lots of them. His mom and dad didn't talk about the medical bills, but he could see the concern on their faces when they opened the envelopes. Carl's mom used to be able to work sometimes, leaving Carl and his three older sisters for a few hours at a time while she went to clean houses in the valley. Because of Carl's illness, she could do this no longer. Carl's dad was a construction worker who went from job to job, taking the work when it came. He worked long hours, driving around in his old truck, with the tools rattling in their box on the back seat. He worked hard, but making ends meet was a struggle.

It had been early September when the polio struck, and Carl had remained very sick until the following February. Once he was well enough to notice, he discovered that he had been ill all through Christmas. There hadn't even been any presents. His mom and dad had turned still and silent when he asked about it, and he hadn't asked again.

Missing Christmas made Carl very sad indeed. He loved Christmas. It was his favorite time of the year. He especially loved the way the family Christmas tree lit up the dark wooden walls of their hillside cabin. He didn't mind missing school—a tutor from the county came in twice a week to catch him up on his lessons—but having missed Christmas was often on his mind.

The long year passed.

* * * * *

Carl was more mobile by the time the next Christmas rolled around. His withered leg was still of little use, but he could put some weight on it without too much pain, and his mom had sewed a soft pillow onto the armrest of his crutch, so it no longer caused blisters as he walked. He could go outside again and say hello to the animals. They flocked around him just as if he were a long-lost friend, which indeed he was—not only to the finches, but also to the squirrels, the possums, and the cats that roamed the shed and kept the mice away.

Carl's home was on a narrow bluff, high up on the side of a steep hill. From his front porch, he could see the whole valley. On his first visit outside in months, he breathed in the crisp air. It gave him energy. He dug his crutch into the snow until it found solid ground and worked his way across the yard, passing the tall fir tree that grew at the front of the property, and looked down the hill at the tiny houses in the town below. A brightly colored bird flew from a branch above and landed on Carl's shoulder. He recognized it as a titmouse. It pecked gently at his ear. For the first time since he had become ill, Carl felt truly happy.

That night, though, at dinner, Carl's dad gave him some sad news.

"We won't have much of a Christmas this year, and I'm truly sorry about that, Son," he said, his deep brown eyes looking concerned. He knew how much his son was looking forward to Christmas.

There would be no presents, except what they could make themselves. No big dinner, except what they could catch—which would make it pretty much like every other meal. His family had always been poor. He never expected expensive gifts or rich food. However, the saddest news of all was that there would be no tree.

"Trees cost money, Son," said Carl's dad, "and then you have to decorate them. This isn't our land—we lease it, you know—and the landowner just gave me a long lecture about cutting down his trees without permission."

Carl was sad, but he attempted to hide it. He knew that his parents worked hard and that they were doing their best. He tried to be cheerful, but as the days grew shorter and the harsh winds of winter could be felt through the thin walls of the tiny cabin, he thought to himself that if it was going to be so dark and dreary, it might just as well not be Christmas at all.

Then, the day before Christmas Eve, Carl's dad came home with a surprise. "The man in the store was throwing them away," he said, holding out a small box. "Damaged, supposedly, but they light up all right. People are just too picky. That's what I think."

He opened the box. Inside was a long wire with numerous tiny bulbs attached.

"Christmas tree lights!" gasped Carl. He looked up at his dad with shining eyes.

"I thought we could put them up there," said Carl's dad, nodding at the big fir tree in the front yard. "I have that long extension cable, so we can hook them up to the socket inside the shed."

Carl picked up his crutch, made his way onto the front porch, and looked up at the huge Douglas fir that stood right outside their house. His dad followed him out and stared at the tree too.

It was massive. Up at the top, there was a smaller bough. Damaged in a storm, it had repaired itself, growing at a slight angle to the rest of the tree. The crooked part had grown out at an odd angle, and Carl realized it was almost a small tree in its own right—just the size of a Christmas tree.

"The wonderful thing about a tree," Carl's dad said as he looked up at the Douglas fir, "is that it's beautiful, no matter what breaks off, no matter how many contortions any of its branches make."

"What if we put the lights on that part, Dad?" said Carl, pointing up at the errant limb.

Carl's dad laughed. "That's way too high, Son," he said. "I don't have a ladder that high, and I'm way too heavy to climb out onto that little branch."

Carl looked up at the tree. At that moment, a light wind blew, and the high branches swayed gently. He heard a faint chirping noise and saw one of the small finches—one of the ones that had learned to fly while he was ill—perched on a narrow offshoot in the highest part of the crooked limb. Both the bird and the tree seemed for a moment to be calling to him.

Carl looked at his dad. "I could climb up there," he said.

Carl's dad almost laughed and started to mouth the words "No way," but he thought better of it. He was about to fetch the ladder and the extension cable and put the lights on the lower part of the tree, but then a bird sang out and something in his son's serious face stopped him.

"It's too dangerous," he said in a soft voice.

"I can do it, Dad," said Carl. Suddenly it had become very important that he climb the tree. "I'm a really good climber. You know that."

"Yes, Son, but that was before..." Carl's dad's eyes tilted toward his son's leg, but he didn't say the words that were on his mind.

"You always say I should just get on with things," said Carl. "You told me about people who have learned to swim without any legs at all. You don't just use your legs to climb. You know that. I have both my arms and my other leg. I can do it. I'll be careful, Dad."

Carl's dad never could figure out how he came to speak the words that came out of his mouth next: "Don't tell your mother."

37

Why in the world had he agreed to what seemed like an insane suggestion? Perhaps something in the wind—a song from one of the birds, maybe—had told him that his son needed this, assured him that if Carl could do this one thing, his withered leg would never stop him from doing anything he wanted to do.

* * * * *

In the morning, on Christmas Eve, Carl's dad fetched the extension cable from his truck and plugged it into the socket in the shed. He unwound the cable until it stretched to its full length of 200 feet. Dressed in a warm wool sweater, Carl strapped his dad's work belt around his waist. He hooked the cable onto one side and the ring of Christmas lights onto the other.

Carl's dad gave him a brief hug. "You can do it, Son," he said. And somehow—he couldn't have told you how—he knew Carl could.

Carl stretched out his arms and pulled himself onto the lower limbs of the tree. Already he felt the effects of the wind, but it was exhilarating to be off of the ground.

The first few branches were the most difficult. Carl was still weak from his long illness, and of course, he had been used to putting weight on both of his legs as he climbed. Not long after he started, he wanted to give up. Out of breath and in pain, he stopped, his hands clasped around the thick trunk.

Then Carl heard a rustle above his head. Looking up, he saw a pair of bright eyes. It was a squirrel. It was watching him closely from a branch several feet above his head. Its nose twitched, and it seemed to be trying to communicate something.

Carl took a deep breath and moved toward the squirrel, grabbing the branches with his arms and using his good leg for support. When he had almost reached the squirrel, it jumped suddenly to a different branch several feet higher and slightly to his left. From its new perch, the squirrel continued to twitch its nose and chat to him in its own special language. Carl heaved his body in the squirrel's direction again, and once again the squirrel moved away before he could reach it.

It eventually dawned on Carl what the squirrel was doing. It was guiding him, showing him the best route to take in order to use the strongest branches. With the squirrel's help, he managed to make his way up through the tree a little bit at a time.

It was still hard work, though. By the time he reached the top of the tree—the point where the high branch jutted out at an angle—Carl was exhausted. He sat on one of the lightly swaying branches and took a rest.

Carl was very high up now. He could see the roof of his cabin below him on his left, and looking to his right, he took in the curve of the hillside as it ran down to the valley below. After a few moments of rest, he unwound the cable of Christmas tree lights and began to arrange them on the branch. At one point, this involved leaning forward quite far in order to reach the tip. He felt the branch creak beneath his body and held his breath, fearing the menacing sound of cracking wood and trying not to think of the steep drop below.

But the branch held. Carl wedged the end of the extension cable between two branches and plugged the lights in. They lit up immediately. Even in daylight, the frosted glass sparkled and warmed Carl's heart. Finally, it was a Christmas tree.

"If only," he thought, "I had a few more decorations for it."

Carl stayed at the top of the tree to rest a bit more before his climb down. As he sat with his head against one of the stronger branches, he noticed a sizeable group of birds clustered around him. They had gathered around the crooked limb, and several of them seemed to be examining the lights. He became concerned that they might peck through the wires and injure themselves.

But then the birds left the tree. For a minute or so, there was silence, but then the birds began to return. They landed on the offshoots of the twisted limb, and Carl could see that each of them had a tiny object in its mouth. Some carried small sprigs of holly, while others brought colorful leaves or pine cones. The birds arranged these objects on the newly illuminated branches.

Could they be doing it on purpose? Carl didn't know for sure. All he knew was that when they were done, the Christmas tree was as colorful and pretty as any he had ever seen in a department store window.

"Thank you," he whispered to the birds. It was growing colder now. The sun was dipping down toward the horizon. Carefully and slowly, Carl climbed back down the tree.

When it became dark, Carl's family came and stood on the porch. At the top of the fir tree, the Christmas tree shone. The frosty lights sparkled, and the birds' decorations caught their glow. Carl's dad hugged him and thanked him for their Christmas tree.

"Thank the animals, too," he said.

Carl's dad smiled when he heard this. He didn't think the animals could really have helped his son climb the tree and decorate it, but he felt thankful for Carl and for the love of his family.

Down in the valley, the people of Grindleaf, West Virginia looked out and saw the glowing, angled Christmas tree next to the Crawdie house. As they looked, they felt the warmth of a new Christmas descend on them through the sharp, cold night. Each person who saw the crooked tree, blazing with light and warmth, felt a little closer to their loved ones that night, and no matter what troubles happened to be facing them, they felt a little more hopeful for the future—and a little more grateful.

"I will honor Christmas in my heart,
and try to keep it all the year."

—CHARLES DICKENS

THE
TALL VIEW

*"There's nothing more contagious
than the dignity of a father."*

—AMIT RAY

Late one summer afternoon, when I was eleven, my father
and I were out walking around the borders of our cornfield, talking about baseball in general and the Chicago Cubs
in particular—my two favorite topics—when I happened to

mention that I had decided I wanted to become a major-league baseball player.

My dad stopped short. There was a long silence. Then he gestured with a sweeping motion of his hand out toward the cornfield and said: "What do you notice out there?"

I shrugged my shoulders. "Corn?" I replied.

His grimace told me that wasn't the answer he was looking for. I looked out again at the vast expanse of yellow and green and ochre—we were on a little hill that gave us a great view—but I didn't notice anything particularly unusual.

"What am I looking for, Dad?" I asked.

"All those stalks of corn. Are they identical?"

"I guess. If you've seen one stalk of corn, you've seen them all."

"Are you sure? Look closer."

I scanned the field again in the fading, slanting afternoon sun, but I still couldn't figure out what in the world my father was talking about. The cornfield was just ... a cornfield. After a minute of increasingly awkward silence, he took pity on me and pointed at a particular stalk of corn.

"There. Right there. You see the top of that stalk of corn?"

"Yes."

"You can count the tassels, can't you?"

I could. There were four of them.

"Yes."

"*Why* can you count them?"

"Because they're standing up higher than the ones on the stalks around them."

"Exactly," my father said. "Exactly." And he stared out at the cornfield.

There was another long silence, but this time I could tell that the pause meant there was something important that he wanted to say to me. This kind of silence only happened when we were alone, and it only happened when he had a point to pass along. Don't ask me how I'd learned to recognize that habit, but I had, and this was definitely one of those silences.

My father looked at me and said, "I never told you this, son, but I spent four years of my life working to make it to the big leagues. I was a shortstop. I was an all-star in the Tacoma League for one year. I played for the Yakima Scouts. I hit .301 that year. This was all before I met your mother, of course."

I was speechless. I couldn't even manage a "Wow." The idea of my father as a professional ballplayer was astounding. I understood now why his interest in the game of baseball ran so deep.

"The next year, though," he went on, "I had a tough injury during the winter, while I was working out at the gym, and I tried to come back too early. My numbers were off in spring training. I got cut. Word got around that I was finished. I didn't think I was finished, but the scouts seemed to think so. I started playing semi-pro ball. I wanted to make it back onto the big-league ladder."

"What happened?"

"Well, I started out fine. Once I was healthy again, I started tearing up the pitching in the semi-pro league. One night, I called up my old manager in the Tacoma League, and I mentioned casually to him that I was leading my new league in average, runs batted in, and stolen bases. In other words, my recovery was complete. I asked him for my old job back."

"What did he say?"

My father swallowed hard, and I thought I saw his eyes begin to water. He turned away quickly, though, so I couldn't be sure. He was staring out at the cornfield again.

"He asked me if he could level with me—tell me the truth about my career."

"And what did you say?"

"I said, 'Sure, Skipper. Level with me.'"

"So did he?"

"He told me the best truth he had, I guess."

"And what was that, Dad?"

"He said I should know that I was too short for the major leagues. He said there had never, ever been a player who made it out of Triple-A who was my height—five foot four—and that he didn't want to see me wasting my life trying. He said he'd talked to half-a-dozen big-league scouts about it—about me. And all of them came back with the exact same verdict. It didn't matter how good my average was, how many bases I stole, or how many runs I knocked in. I wasn't going to make it past Triple-A, because I was too short. And I believed him."

My dad sniffed hard, wiped something from his eye, and stared out at the cornfield.

"I guess that must have been the worst day of your life."

"Actually, no. That's what I thought at first. But it wasn't. The worst day of my life came three years later, after I'd been out of baseball for far too long, gained too much weight, and hurt my throwing hand for good working on a tractor engine."

I could see my dad's right hand as he spoke, with the long, dense scar that ran along the length of his inner thumb and across his palm. I had grown used to that scar, and to my father's reliance upon his left hand. His being left-handed—and the fact that it wasn't by choice—had become something of a family joke over the years. My mom called him "Lefty" sometimes when they were both relaxed enough for him to laugh about it. But the scar didn't seem all that funny now.

"The worst day of my life came when I read that Freddie Patek had been signed to a contract with the Kansas City Royals. Freddie came up the year after I quit pro ball. He was five foot three and a half—a little shorter than me."

My dad was silent for a while. He seemed to be gathering his thoughts. Then he continued: "I saw an interview with Freddie Patek on TV just after he got signed. He was pretty newsworthy right about then, because he was the shortest man ever signed to a major-league contract. The reporter asked him what the key to his success was. He said that every time someone questioned his ability or his commitment to achieve his goal—a scout, a manager, anybody—he just remembered that his job was to do his best and stand a little taller than any problem that came his way. He said that if he stood tall and let God handle the rest, he could be happy with himself, regardless of the outcome."

My dad shook his head briskly, as if to shake himself free of the memory, then turned to face me.

"I want you to know something, Jimmy. I don't regret anything that has happened to me in my life. I'm happy with what God has given me. I'm happy to be a farmer now. But I do regret some of my choices. That's the way it is in life. You make choices, and sometimes, you realize you made the wrong ones. The reason I'm telling you this now is that I don't want you to make the same kind of bad choice I did."

"How do you mean?"

"Well, Son, I'm glad you want to be a big leaguer. I'd been hoping you'd say something like that, of your own accord. And I'd love to try to help you get there if you want. But you need to know something. Years ago, I made myself a promise about you. And I intend to keep it."

"What promise was that?"

"I swore to myself that if you ever told me you wanted to be a pro ballplayer, I'd share with you the lesson I learned on the worst day of my life."

He was looking deep into my eyes now.

"Jimmy, you noticed that stalk of corn because it stood out. It was Freddie Patek. And you didn't notice all the other stalks of corn because they didn't stand out. They were me."

He made another gesture out toward the cornfield, and I could tell he wanted me to study that cornstalk again.

"Freddie Patek took the tall view—and I could have, too, but I didn't. That's what happened. I can't change it now. This is what I learned, though: No matter how tall you are, you have to stand tall. You owe that to yourself. Back when I made that call to my manager, I stopped standing tall. I stopped trying, stopped believing in myself. I accepted someone else's definition of what my potential was, Jimmy, and I've been living with that bad decision ever since. A day hasn't gone by that I haven't thought about my choice to give up early on my baseball career. Now, I want you to know that I'll never, ever be disappointed in you if you don't manage to make it to the big leagues. I'll never be disappointed in you for trying hard and failing. But I *will* be disappointed in you if you ever let someone talk you into not standing tall. Can you promise me you'll stand tall, no matter what you run up against in life—whether it's in baseball or out of it?"

I promised. And while I never made it to the big leagues, I made my father proud trying. I never, ever, sold myself short. I took the tall view. And that choice has made both of us happier, better, and more grateful men.

"Continuous effort—not strength or intelligence—
is the key to unlocking our potential."

—WINSTON CHURCHILL

Take
My Hand

"Blessed is the one who trusts in the Lord."

—Psalm 40:4a

His dad was not an emotionally expressive or affectionate man with his family. His dad was tough, and at times, quite disapproving, often at the very moment his son most felt the need for his approval.

His dad was extremely devoted to his work. Today, in fact,

we might call him a workaholic. Back then, people called such a man a good provider, and there is some truth to both labels. Whatever we choose to call it, the reality was that he spent most of his time in the grocery shop below their apartment, and the son saw very little of him, even though he was only a few steps away.

Just as the dad had been, the son was a restless middle child who stood in the shadow of the firstborn son. As he entered adolescence, the son began to feel a disconnection from his family and the sensation of being deeply alone. That feeling of disconnection and loneliness led to a great deal of pain, and he began looking around for ways to dull that pain.

He found one way to dull the pain—or at least he thought he did—with a rough gang of older boys with whom he began drinking heavily at the age of thirteen. There was a lot of talk in the newspapers during this period about a social problem called "juvenile delinquency." Truth be told, the son was probably part of that problem. He got into the habit of drinking beer either right before or after school. This habit lasted for years.

Everyone in his family knew that he wasn't doing well in school and that he had fallen in with a bad crowd. That was certainly true, but it was also true that something much more serious had happened. His whole life was headed in a bad direction. They didn't know how bad yet, and he didn't, either.

He called the bunch of rowdy guys that he hung out with "the Warriors." Most of them were older than he was. They all had problems at home of various kinds. In a way, their group served as each one's alternate family. The instinct to gather together with others who shared one's problems was understandable— it's the same instinct that drives problems with gangs in big cities today. When young men feel alienated and disconnected, and they don't have a lot of support from their families, they reach out to each other for support. There's nothing wrong with any of that in theory, but sometimes the ways that guys find to support each other don't actually end up giving much support to anyone.

That's the way it was with the Warriors. They were fighting a losing battle. Their recreation was bad for them and bad for everyone it touched.

He was a big part of making that recreation happen, as it turned out, because he knew how to drive. He was big for his age—six foot one by the time he was thirteen—and if he didn't talk much, people actually thought he was grown up. That meant he could get the Warriors to the liquor store (driving someone else's car, of course), and he could also pass for eighteen, which was how old you had to be to buy liquor. So he was a pretty useful guy to have around.

The Warriors drank a lot of beer, because beer was cheap. On special occasions—which is another way of saying whenever somebody had a few extra bucks—the Warriors drank whiskey. He never drank alone. He always drank with the Warriors. He felt at home with the Warriors.

His dad had never been a drinker. In fact, except for an occasional glass of wine, alcohol was off limits in his dad's house. That might have even been part of the reason it was important to him to spend as much time out drinking with the Warriors as he did.

The Warriors drank too much, and they did it most nights of the week. They drank at someone's house if they knew the parents were away. They drank in the car if they couldn't find anywhere else. Somehow, he was always the guy doing the driving—without a license, of course—and half of the time he had had too much to drink when he drove. He never stopped to ask himself what accounted for the miracle that kept him from getting hurt or killed on those binge outings. The Warriors operated on the assumption that nothing bad could happen to any of them.

One night, as he drove drunk through a hayfield, he opened the window and shouted, "The Warriors are invincible!" All the Warriors in the back seat laughed at that, which was an odd way of agreeing with him, but that's what they were doing.

By the time he was fourteen, drinking with his friends had become a way of life. Ultimately, it was a sad way of life—a way that usually left him feeling terrible the next morning—but at least he always had a party he could look forward to and a group that gave him a feeling of belonging somewhere. The Warriors raised a ruckus more or less every night, and there was not a thing any adult could do or say about it. That was just how it was. His grades had collapsed, and his family was growing more distant by the day, but at least he belonged somewhere—or thought he did.

But as long as there have been beer-drinking boys driving around in cars, there have been dangers waiting for them at night, and the biggest problem comes when danger begins to looks like opportunity.

The night when everything began to unravel for the Warriors began like any other. It started with beer—and plenty of it. He and his friends got together and chipped in a few bucks each. He bought the beer. They spent the better part of the evening drinking in the car on a secluded country road. Then they decided to devote the remainder of the night to driving around so they could see what was going on in the great, spinning world that lay before them. He was behind the wheel of his best friend's dad's Chevy, and he felt invincible again. They all did.

As it turned out, what was going on in the town was that a large fire had broken out at a sporting goods store. They could see where the flames must have been howling out of the openings of the building not too long before, but they had been put out by now. A big front window had been broken somehow, probably by the firefighters. He parked the car so the Warriors could get out and take a look.

Now, if you take a bunch of teenage boys who have been drinking too much and show them a store that has just been burned in a fire, there's a couple of interesting things that may happen. If it had been a really intense fire, and if the boys aren't particularly imaginative, they may just stare for a while in awe and wait for the fire department or the police to come back (as of course they will), and then the boys will realize that it's time to head home before anyone starts asking them awkward questions. But if you've got a group of real visionary thinkers like the ones that had gathered in that car that night—if you've got, in short, the Warriors—then a whole different and much more interesting avenue for strategic planning develops. People start thinking about whether they should help themselves to the goods in the blackened store.

No mind on earth could have determined whose idea that was—it might have been his—but once it had been spoken out loud, everyone seemed to think it was brilliant.

What difference did it make? All of the stuff in the store was going to be replaced by insurance money anyway. The firefighters had already secured the place. The police were nowhere to be seen. They could help themselves. What could possibly go wrong?

The Warriors stumbled, laughing, out of the car.

Through a back door that looked like it must have been hacked open with the axes of the firefighters, they surged into the blackened, smoldering building and started helping themselves to water-soaked, singed, and soot-covered pocket knives, catcher's mitts, footballs, and any number of other damaged items that could be of interest to them. They had had just enough to drink to consider themselves very lucky indeed.

They were having a grand time, laughing and joking and generally enjoying themselves at the expense of the rest of the world, competing with one another for who could pick out most impressive stuff.

He said it was the best night out yet. All the Warriors laughed and agreed with him.

Then they saw the flashing red light and heard the words of someone—presumably someone in uniform—saying, "Police! All of you, stop where you are and turn around right now!"

If there was any doubt in their minds or hearts about whether or not anything could possibly go wrong that night, it vanished in that moment. There was also, as it turned out, no doubt whatsoever about whether or not any of them wanted to be arrested. They all wanted to be out of there in a hurry.

They ignored the unseen officer's helpful instructions, dropped everything that they had gathered, turned, and ran for the back door like coon dogs that had just picked up the scent. They must have gotten out of the hacked-open back door in less than a second.

Somehow, distracted and terrified as he was, things suddenly became quite clear for him—and for all of the Warriors. They all decided simultaneously, without a word, that their best chance for escaping disaster lay in abandoning the car and separating as quickly as possible. Each of them sped off on foot in separate directions, fueled by the combustible mix of adrenaline, fear, the night, and the looming possibility of being thrown in jail. He ran into the darkness, as only a teenage boy who knows that trouble is right behind him can run.

He knew that directly behind the department store, down a steep embankment, was a weed-filled body of water—a canal—and he found himself on a neglected, overgrown road that led straight to it. Intuitively, he followed that road, and his mind began to churn as his strong, young, terrified legs carried him forward.

Horses no longer trotted along this road, and barges no longer used the canal to bring cotton or newspapers or lumber from one point to another. In the half-century since the advent of the automobile, the canal had become an open sewer. No longer needed as a freight artery, it was now a convenient place to dump waste, human and otherwise. People didn't much care where they dumped their waste, and companies didn't much care about the environmental impact of heaving all kinds of garbage, some of it pretty disgusting, into the canal. The once-proud highway of commerce had become a fetid river of muck, mire, and sewage. And it smelled to high heaven.

Just a few seconds after he bolted out the back door of the sporting goods store, he picked up the canal's distinctive scent. Now, as the vile odor got stronger, he formed an idea.

What was the last place in the world that anyone—even a police officer—would want to go into in search of a wayward teen who had clearly recognized the error of his ways?

He knew the answer: The dark, stinking waters of the canal that had grown into a sewer.

He skidded down the embankment, closed his lips tight, held his nose, and got ready to take the single worst swim of his life.

Before five seconds had passed, he was up to his chest in sewer water. Hunks of waste floated past him. The whole thing smelled awful. And now he did too. But surely he was well out of sight of the police.

A large bridge spanned the canal. Alongside the canal ran some railroad tracks. A train passed and blew its whistle, and he wished he was on it. But he wasn't. A few long moments went by and then—the worst sight in the world. Through the gloom, he could see exactly what he was afraid he would see: Three officers at the top of that bridge, shining the broad beams of three flashlights into the depths of the water.

He made his way, just as quickly as he could, over toward a bank that gave him cover behind some tall reeds. It seemed out-of-the-way and beyond the reach of those flashlights. He was still chest-deep in filth. At least here, he could hide behind the reeds. He heard the low, distant voices of the police as they conferred with one another, but he could not make out any of their words. They seemed insistent, whatever they were. He wasn't sure how they could see much of anything in the strange darkness that surrounded him that evening.

The stench of the water was overpowering. He wondered if he would pass out. He thought that if he passed out, he'd likely fall face-first into the muck, and perhaps drown and die in it—a terrible way to meet his end—and he resolved to maintain consciousness. At that instant he realized he was probably the least invincible person on the face of the earth.

Surrounded—and not only by the dense mire of waste—he tried not to move and not to make a sound. If the police came wading into the filth to track him down, he was done for. He would never see his family again. On the other hand, if he was more patient than they were, if he was quiet, and if he had bet right that they were unwilling to sacrifice their time, their dignity, and their uniforms hunting down a wayward teenage boy in a river of filth, then he was safe.

A loud, husky-voiced police officer called from the bridge. There was no use in him hiding. They would find him sooner or later. It would all be easier for him if he came out now and talked to them.

He felt his heart pounding in his chest. And at that moment he did something that he could not recall ever having done before: He prayed with all his heart for help from God the Father.

Of course, he had never been in a spot as difficult as this one before, and what he was praying for—not to be punished for something that he had done that was clearly wrong, even to him—was not all that noble. It is possible, too, that the fear in his heart was less a fear of God than it was a fear of what his father would say and do if he ever found out about the fix he had gotten himself into. Despite all of this, or perhaps because of it, he continued to pray with every atom of his being for God to see him safely through this horrific set of circumstances.

His prayer was for help from God the Father—if he was really there. He was honest enough to admit at that moment that he didn't really know. He pleaded for an answer anyway.

He prayed for a way forward. If only God would make him safe in this terrible situation, he promised, he would never fall this far again, and he would strive to be a better son, a better Christian, and a better person—a better anything—as long as he could get out of these weeds tonight without going to jail.

To his astonishment, there came an answer.

The clear answer that came to him in his hiding place in the muck and mire, came not in spoken words, but in thoughts planted into his very being. The answer could not have been perceived audibly by others, perhaps, but it was audible in his heart and in his mind.

The words of the answer he received were, "Take my hand," and he understood those words perfectly. All of a sudden, there was possibility. There was hope. There was a way forward. He had no idea what it was exactly, but he knew, in the marrow of his bones, that it existed.

But then, just a fraction of a second later, another thought entered his mind. It was an opposing voice, an oppressive voice, a voice that told him, "There is no hope. You are no good. You are lost. You have failed your family."

That negative voice pulled him down. Again he felt doomed and hopeless, beyond redemption and beyond forgiveness. His foot slipped on something, and he made a splash and could not right himself. He could feel himself slipping down further into the muck and mire of his own life. The flashlights on the bridge circled and swung, looking for the source of the noise.

Then he heard again these words from the Father God: "Take my hand!"

He did. In his mind's eye, he saw a hand being extended toward him, and he grabbed that hand, steadied himself, and held on tightly. At that moment, the police officers flicked off their flashlights. He heard their footsteps walking away, and he knew they had—for the moment at least—called off their search.

His eyes had adjusted to the darkness. It was time to make his way out of the canal.

Years later, he learned from a friend that the opposing voice is always present in our minds, always trying to drag us down, always trying to get us to stray from the path that God wants to see us on. It is the voice of *sarx*—the Greek word that can be translated as "the flesh" or "the old nature." This same friend explained further that, in any given moment, we must choose whom we will listen to in life. He used the illustration of the Continental Divide: If we stand at the peak of the divide and pour water down one side of it, it will flow to the Atlantic Ocean. If we choose to pour it down the opposite side, it will flow to the Pacific. It's all a matter of which direction we choose. In the same way, we must each choose whom we will listen to: The voice that calls us to the way of life or the one that leads us toward the path of darkness.

A verse of Scripture that his mother often read to him perfectly summed up his experience that evening:

I waited patiently for the Lord; He turned to me and heard my cry. He lifted me out of the slimy pit, out of the muck and mire; he set my feet on a firm place to stand. He put a new song in my mouth, a hymn of praise to our God. Many will see and fear the Lord and put their trust in Him. Blessed is the one who trusts in the Lord. (Psalm 40:1b-4a)

As he drew himself out of the filth, he realized how tired he was of his own foolish ways, of the path he had chosen, of the choices that had brought him to this horrible place. He was ready to listen, ready to pray more about how to improve his own condition, ready to ask for help from God—help in becoming the person God wanted him to be. At that moment, he knew that God existed. Stepping from the depths of the muck and mire, he knew he had to turn things around. If he somehow got out of this, he had to make sure things changed.

His prayer had been answered, but like many prayers, it was answered in a way that would take a while for him to understand. At the moment, all he knew was that he was free. Smelly, wet, and exhausted, but free. He was black with sewage, covered from head to foot in filth. After taking a short, cleansing dip, clothes and all, in the clean running water of a nearby creek, he felt strangely refreshed in body, mind and spirit. As he found his way home that evening, he thought of his father without fear, doubt, or anxiety. He did not know what he would say to his father, and he did not know what would become of him. But he knew that he was going home, where he belonged, he knew that God would guide his steps, and he was grateful.

Faith is taking the first step, even when you don't see the whole staircase.

—MARTIN LUTHER KING, JR.

THE
COPPER MINE

Remember then—there is only one time that is
important: Now! It is the most important time because
it is the only time over which we have any power.

—LEO TOLSTOY

Growing up, my dad always kept a small wooden box on the mantelpiece. I was curious about that box. It was made out of inexpensive wood, and it had a tiny bird carved roughly into the surface. My dad said it was a canary.

"What's in the box, Dad?" I asked when I was seven years old.

Something in his face changed. His eyes grew narrow, like they did when he was angry, but he gave me a sad smile I hadn't seen before. "There's a story about that box," he said. "I'll tell you, when you're old enough."

At my next birthday, I asked, "Am I old enough yet, Dad?"

He smiled an odd kind of grim smile. "Not yet," he answered.

I asked again on my next birthday and the next, but it was not until I was 11 that my father took down the box from the mantelpiece and opened it with a tiny key.

Inside was a little tool, kind of like a miniature hammer. I had been expecting the box to be full of treasures, so I was a little disappointed, and it must have shown on my face, because my father said, "Disappointed, are you?"

I shook my head, but my face must have shown otherwise.

"It's understandable," he said. "One man's treasure is another man's trash."

"You said you'd tell me the story."

"Yes," he said. There was a long pause. "I will."

"The first real job I ever got," Dad said, "was in a copper mine. I was paid fairly well—it was more than most 19-year-olds got, so I was pleased and proud to get it. But when I told my mother about it, she was upset. 'People get killed in the mines,' she said. 'There have been accidents.'

"'I won't get killed, Mom,' I said. 'Don't worry. I'll be careful.'

"I was careful. But the job was very difficult. I spent long days beneath the ground. When I came up out of the mines each evening, it was dark.

"I missed the sunlight. The endless days without it made me feel bad. Jokes that had once seemed funny no longer made me laugh. On my rare days off, I would often stay in bed, watching the rays of sunlight coming in the window but not going out to enjoy them.

"One thing made it almost bearable—or I should say, one person. That was Jonah. Jonah worked on the same shift as me. He had been working in the copper mines for a long time. His skin was pasty white from the lack of sunlight, but the work did not get to him the way it did to me. He talked from one end of the day to the other. He was a repository of stories, jokes, and songs.

"It was near the end of our shift that it happened. Jonah and I were on our own in the tunnel. He was ahead of me, pushing the cart full of copper ore. I was holding the canary in its cage."

"The canary, Dad?" I asked. "Why did you have a canary?"

"Well," he said. "Canaries die very quickly if the air goes bad.

Much faster than humans. Miners carry canaries so they have a warning if the oxygen starts to run out."

"Poor canaries," I said.

"Yes," he said. "Our canary was called Theseus. He was very loud. Sang all the time. Between him and Jonah, I got no peace. We almost didn't hear the explosion when it happened."

"Explosion!?" I gasped.

"Yes. It was a dull sound," Dad said. "And it sounded very far away. A thud. As if someone had dropped something. Then there was another sound, like an echo. But it got louder and closer, and then the whole tunnel collapsed around us. I blacked out. I don't know for how long. But when I woke up, it was pitch dark and I couldn't move. The walls had fallen in on us, you see.

"For a while, I just lay there. I was terrified—sure that I was going to die alone in the darkness. I thought of my mother and my promise that I would be safe. I felt terribly guilty for breaking that promise.

"Then I heard a sound. It was Theseus, the canary, singing. I can't tell you how happy that made me. I talked back at him and he sang even more.

"Then there was the sound of a match striking, and a light appeared. It made the cavern glow. It was Jonah, holding a lamp. He was crouched nearby. He had blood running down his face where a piece of sharp rock had hit him, but amazingly he managed to smile at me."

"'So you're alive,' he said.

"I looked around. Most of the tunnel was gone. The space where we were trapped was no more than a few square feet. Unless we were rescued very quickly, the oxygen would run out. We would not survive.

"'I think this is it, Jonah,' I said.

"'No,' he said. 'They'll find us.'

"I tried to move. A burst of pain shot up my leg. 'I'm injured, Jonah,' I said. 'I can't move my legs.'

"He crawled closer, examining the rocks around my legs by the light of the lamp. 'It's just these rocks,' he said. 'When they're cleared, your leg will be fine.'

"I noticed that the cut on his head seemed very deep. Blood was trickling down from his hair and landing on his chest. 'You need a bandage,' I said. I felt in my pocket and found a handkerchief. It was clean. I tore it up and helped Jonah to tie it around his head. The blood flow eased.

"Theseus gave a small chirp. It occurred to me that he had stopped singing. He stood on his perch in the cage, turning his head quickly from one side to the other. 'We should put out the lamp,' I said to Jonah. 'The air will go bad more quickly if we don't.' His expression grew grim. Neither of us wanted to return to darkness. But he nodded.

'Should we call out?' I asked some time later.

"Jonah shook his head. 'We could cause a rock fall. This is what we do.' He reached into his jacket pocket and took out his small mining hammer. 'We tap the walls. We keep tapping. They'll be looking. They'll find us. You'll see.'

"Jonah blew out the lamp and we were plunged into darkness once again. Theseus gave a mournful cheep as Jonah began to tap at the stones nearby. I took out my own mining hammer and did the same. Tap, tap, tap. We tapped endlessly.

"Theseus grew quiet in the dark. Every now and then, I would give the cage bars a tiny shake. It was almost a relief to hear the small chirp in response. As long as Theseus was alive, we knew we could breathe safely.

"The air grew cold in the cavern—or maybe the warmth was vanishing from my body. It was hard to tell. Eventually Jonah said, 'I'm worn out. I need to rest. We should take turns tapping.' So we took turns. Jonah fell asleep. I could hear his rough breathing. It did not sound good. Later, Jonah tapped and I tried to sleep, but it was a strange kind of sleep. Even though I dreamed, I never seemed to leave the cavern.

"Time passed. In the darkness, it was impossible to know how much time. Each of us would tap the walls until we became weary. While I tapped, Jonah sometimes slept. At other times, he would talk to me, tell me stories. At one point I heard a scraping noise.

"'Is someone coming?' I asked.

"He sighed. 'No. Sorry, pal. That's just me. I found this bit of wood and I was carving a picture of Theseus into it.'

"'I didn't know you could carve,' I said.

"'I can,' he replied. 'Pretty well, in daylight. But in the dark, who can tell? It might not look like a bird at all.'

"The scraping noise went on for some time. Then, Jonah fell asleep. I tapped at the wall and listened to his rasping breath. Occasionally he would stop breathing altogether. I would sit there, fearfully waiting for the inevitable choking sound as his breath was drawn once more into his lungs. It seemed that the gaps between the breaths were getting longer and longer.

"When he woke, he offered to tap, but I did not feel like resting. The rhythm of tapping was keeping me sane. Jonah began to carve once again. Eventually, he said, 'All done, I think. Here.' He handed me the piece of wood. 'What do you think?'

"I ran my hand over the carving. It felt like a bird. 'It's good,' I said.

"I reached out to hand it back, but he said, 'You have it, Bill. It's yours. You can have it to remember me by, after you are rescued.'

"I still remember Jonah's voice, echoing through the cavern as he said these words. And he was right. A while later, he fell asleep again. And after one long, rasping, painful breath, he did not breathe again. Alone in the darkness, I felt panic welling up in me. I jangled the bars of Theseus's cage. The bird did not respond. Maybe the cold had killed him. Or hunger. Or maybe it was the air. There was no way to tell.

"Certain now that I was not going to survive, I tapped the walls again and again.

"Eventually, I heard voices—or at least I thought I did. I had stopped trusting my own senses. Still, disregarding Jonah's advice, I shouted for help. It wasn't long before rescuers arrived with stretchers and warm blankets. I was pulled out of the rubble. When I was carried out into daylight, the first face I recognized was my mother's. The tears were streaming down her face, and she threw her arms around me.

"'Never, ever, go back down a mine again,' she said. I promised that I would not.

"Jonah had been right about my leg. It was broken, but not too badly. Within a few months, I could walk without crutches.

"Time passed. I kept my promise to my mother and took a job in a grocery store. I never worked in a mine again. It was pleasant to be able to see daylight while I worked, and I was happy except for the occasional bad dreams, the ones where I was stuck in a dark space and could hear nothing but the tap, tap, tapping of the hammer.

"I kept Jonah's carving. Years later, your mother suggested that I get it made into a box. I did so, and I put the hammer that had saved my life into it."

"Doesn't it make you feel sad?" I asked my dad.

He placed the hammer back into the box and put it back onto the mantelpiece. "Yes, it does, son," he said, "a little." He sat down on the sofa and put his arm around me. "But it also reminds me of good things," he said. "Of love and friendship. Of how people can help each other. Of the fact that life is short and that we should enjoy the sunshine while we can. That each moment we share with each other is precious. You're old enough to know that now. You're old enough to know we can be grateful for these things if we choose to be."

I looked out of the window at the bright garden beyond. My dad said, "Shall we go out and enjoy some of that sunshine now?" And that's just what we did.

The meeting of two eternities, the past and the future, is precisely the present moment.

—HENRY DAVID THOREAU

THE DREAM OF AMERICA

"Best friends are people who make your problems their problems—just so you don't have to go through them alone."

—ANONYMOUS

When Artur Horvat arrived at Ellis Island in June of 1913, he knew just two English words: work and apple.

He learned the first word before he left his home country, which is now known as Slovenia. At the time, it was part of a country called Yugoslavia. Artur had worked hard on the farm where he grew up. But it was the tradition for the eldest son to inherit the farm, and Artur, who had two older brothers, did not see a future on the land.

In the local cafés where Artur spent some of his free time, people spoke of America as the land of milk and honey. One of his friends had relatives there. "People have so much money, they let it fall in the streets," said Artur's friend. "And anyone can find work. You just have to shout out the word as you get off the boat, and you will get job offers."

"Delo?" said Artur, mouthing the Slovenian word for work.

"Work," said his friend, using the English word. "They call it 'work.'"

When Artur told his parents that he planned to go to America and find work, they were perplexed.

"There is plenty to do here," said his father, gesturing to the sun-bleached vineyards that surrounded their home.

There *was* plenty of work on the farm, Artur knew. But as the third son, he told his parents, he could never make much of his life. "America is the land of opportunity," he said.

Artur learned his second English word on the deck of a ship, as the dim shape of the Statue of Liberty rose up in the foggy air ahead of them. Artur and the other passengers were lined up on deck, watching the busy port. A cargo ship had pulled up ahead of them, and large crates of delicious-looking fruit were being wheeled off it on wheelbarrows. Artur was on speaking terms with one of the other passengers, Ciril. Ciril spoke some English, and Artur asked him how to pronounce the word written on the crate.

"Apple," said Ciril.

"Appos," Artur did his best to repeat.

"No, no, no. It's apple—APPLE."

Artur repeated the word, looking with longing at the fresh, green fruit. He repeated it until he could say it perfectly, all the while wishing he could eat an apple. It had been a long sea journey, and although there had been enough to eat, the food had grown increasingly bland as the voyage went on.

Ciril gave Artur a crisp ten-dollar bill before the two parted. "You should have a little more American money in your pocket before you set foot in America," he said, smiling. Artur hugged the older man and shook his hand, feeling deeply grateful.

An hour later, Artur was on American soil for the first time, giving his details to an immigration officer on Ellis Island, who wrote them down on the thick ledger on the table in front of him.

It was some time before Artur had an opportunity to examine the documents the immigration officer gave him. Only then did he realize that the man had misspelled both of his names. He was now Arthur Hovit. He was to be known as Arthur Hovit for the rest of his life.

When Arthur Hovit emerged onto the streets of New York for the first time, there were two thoughts in his head. One was that his thin jacket was going to be incredibly inadequate in this cold weather, and the other was how much he wanted food—an apple, say. He wished he had learned the American word for food, but he hadn't. He went into the first place he could find that sold food. It was a bakery.

"Apple," he said.

The young woman behind the counter had very pretty chestnut-colored hair. She also had a very nice smile that warmed Arthur's heart. She gestured to him to sit down and, a few minutes later, brought him a steaming plate.

"Apple pie," she said, pointing at it.

To Arthur, after weeks at sea, the apple pie seemed like the nicest thing he had ever tasted.

Those first few weeks were very difficult for Arthur. He knew nobody in New York. He did not speak the language, and he had yet to find the work that everyone had promised him would be so thick on the ground. He had arrived in America with less than twenty dollars, more than half of which had come from Ciril. This represented years of savings in Slovenia, but he knew that his cash would run out if he didn't find work soon. He found a cheap bed in a hostel full of people who all spoke different languages. None of them spoke Slovenian, and Arthur felt very lonely at times. He spent his days walking the streets, knocking on the doors of shops and factories, asking for work. Almost always, the response was a stony shake of the head.

Whenever Arthur was hungry, he would visit a bakery and ask for apple pie. It was his one pleasure, and the hot apple filling warmed him after the long days spent on the icy streets.

One day, Arthur knocked on a door to ask for work and was almost surprised when the grey-haired man who answered did not shake his head. Arthur was gratified to discover that the man spoke Slovenian. It was a joy to be able to speak his own language for the first time in weeks.

"What most people don't realize," the grey-haired man told him, "is that you have to spend money to find work. You need to invest."

The grey-haired man told Arthur of an opportunity he knew of with a friend of his who worked on the docks. "He only gives this chance to people he knows very well," said the man, "so you are very lucky. He knows me well, and he will take you on my recommendation."

Arthur went with his new acquaintance, who said his name was Andrew, to a small office on the side of the docks. There, he was introduced to another man, a much younger man, who wore a rich-looking fur coat. Arthur, shivering in his thin jacket, imagined how warm it must be. The other man spoke quickly in a very soft voice. He did not speak Slovenian, so Andrew translated.

"He says that he has enough people," said Andrew. "He does not really need more. But he is such a good friend of mine that he will help you anyway. First you have to give him the money for your uniform and tools."

Arthur may have felt some misgivings as he handed over almost all that remained of his money, but he was cold and needed work, and the papers that the other man pulled from his bag and asked him to sign looked so professional. He felt sure that the offer was genuine.

Once the papers were signed, the man in the fur coat handed one of them to Arthur and put the rest back into his bag. Then he waved them out of the office.

"He wants you to come here on Monday morning," said Andrew. "He will have your uniform and tools for you then and you can start work."

Of course, when Arthur arrived at the docks on Monday morning, the office was closed. There was no sign of the man in the fur coat. He spent an hour looking for him. Then he walked across town to the building where he had met Andrew. There was no sign of him either.

It took several days before Arthur was sure that he had been cheated. The money he had handed over was gone.

Arthur walked from door to door, asking for work, but people seemed to be repelled by his desperation, and they closed their doors in his face.

One day, cold and hungry, with only a few cents left in his pocket, Arthur found himself outside the bakery he had visited on his very first day in New York. Thoughts of the warm, steaming apple pie, the nicest he had ever tasted, came into his mind. He decided to treat himself one last time.

The girl behind the counter was the same girl as last time. Her chestnut hair was tied up neatly, and she looked as pretty as ever. She recognized Arthur and gave him her warm smile.

"Hello," she said. "Apple pie?"

He nodded, without smiling back, and sat down at a table. The girl seemed to notice his sadness. When she brought the pie, she hesitated for a moment beside him.

"Where are you from?" she asked.

Arthur knew a little more English now and worked out what she meant. He stood up and showed her on a map that was pinned to the wall nearby.

The girl's face lit up. "Wait here," she said.

She went to the door and called up the stairs. Moments later an old woman appeared. Her face was so wrinkled she could have been more than a hundred years old, but she had bright, gleaming eyes. The girl spoke quickly to her, and the old woman turned around and spoke to Arthur in fluent Slovenian.

Arthur later learned that the old woman had been in New York for thirty years. She had started as a maid and then begun work in the bakery. The girl at the counter, Alice, was her grand-daughter. Alice had been born in America and only knew a few words of Slovenian. Nonetheless, with the old woman trans-lating, Arthur told them both all about his experiences since arriving in New York. They were shocked when they learned about the conmen who had stolen his money.

"We will help you," said the old woman. "There is plenty of work, when you look in the right places. You do not have to pay for it—you just have to work hard."

This turned out to be true. Arthur found work with a milliner, who also came from Slovenia. He worked long hours, but his employer was friendly, and at the end of the first week, he was presented with an envelope full of coins.

Arthur went straight to the bakery. Alice smiled at him from behind the counter.

"Apple pie, please," he said.

Arthur worked hard for the milliner and later moved to Illinois, where he set up his own business selling textiles. When he had made enough money, he traveled back to New York and found the bakery where Alice had worked. Standing at the counter, he asked her to marry him.

Alice smiled that warm smile and said yes.

The story of the apple pie was repeated down through the years and became a family tradition. Arthur never forgot the lesson he had learned during those first difficult weeks in America. He taught his children to work hard and never lose hope, to think twice before handing money over to strangers, and to be grateful for every opportunity that came their way.

"Remember, remember always, that all of us, and you and I especially, are descended from immigrants."

—**Franklin D. Roosevelt**

THE PRINTER'S DEVIL

"Gratitude is not merely the greatest of virtues, but the parent of all others."

—CICERO

No one told me how the job got that awful name. To this day, I still don't know.

All I knew was that my mom needed help paying the bills after my father left us. She was too proud to say so, and even though I knew she would never ask me in a million years to pitch in financially, I wanted to help. After all, I was eighteen now and had been out of high school for two whole months. I didn't see any reason on earth why a young man who was sound in mind and body shouldn't earn something to contribute toward household expenses when his mother was putting in eleven-hour days cleaning up hospital messes, which was nasty business. So when my buddy Frankie said, "Mickey, there's an opening for a printer's devil at McMahon Press that pays fifty bucks a week for three hours of your time each day," I said, "Who do I talk to?"

"Don't you even want to know what a printer's devil is?"

"Is the fifty bucks a week paid in American dollars?"

"Yeah."

"The kind my mom can spend at the grocery store?"

"Yeah."

"Does this fellow McMahon pay regularly?"

"Sure he does."

"Then I want the job. I'll figure out the details as I go along."

"Mickey, let me ask you something. Have you ever *had* a job before?"

"Nope. But my mom could sure use the dough."

Frankie must have been able to tell that my mom really was in a tight fix and that I was worried about her, because he didn't ask any more questions. He just said, "Come by the plant tomorrow afternoon, after I get out of school. I'll introduce you to Old Man McMahon. But listen, Mickey. If you do this, do it for real. I don't want my brother to get in trouble because I pointed the wrong kid toward the job. He's had his job at the press for over a year, and he wants to hold onto it."

"I won't let you down, Frankie."

"Now Old Man McMahon is tough, but he's fair. My brother told me all about him. Just be sure to pay attention the whole time you're on the job. McMahon specializes in noticing when you're not noticing. So don't give him any chances to get sore. Got it?"

"Got it."

Frankie's brother Virgil was the one I met first when I showed up at McMahon Press the first day. The press was running, so I could hardly hear what he was yelling at me—something about Old Man McMahon being out for a while, and how I'd better not screw up.

"Frankie already told me," I shouted back.

"What?"

"Frankie already told me about McMahon. I know. Pay attention. Don't let him catch me goofing off."

Virgil seemed almost satisfied with this. He scowled, pointed me toward the break room and said something I couldn't quite catch. I settled in and waited.

Five minutes went by. Then ten. Then thirty. Finally, I figured McMahon must have gotten hung up somewhere, and I decided I could catch up on a little reading. I pulled a folded-up issue of *Superman* out of my lunch box and learned all about Lex Luthor's evil plan to sink Metropolis into the sea by detonating a secret cache of underground nuclear weapons. It was a great issue, and I'd gotten all the way up to page sixteen, where Superman was about to foil the plot by reversing time itself, when a gravelly voice behind me hissed and rumbled the following question:

"So what in blazes did they tell you? Did they tell you a printer's devil is supposed to sit around in the break room all day reading comic books?"

I turned and saw a mountain of a man, sunburned, bald, and ill-favored about the face. He had the deepest wrinkles I had ever seen. He must have been at least seventy years old, maybe eighty. Maybe more.

"Well?"

"No, sir. I'm Mickey Reardon, sir. Frankie said–"

"I know what Frankie said. Your mother's in trouble and you're willing to work. How about we start with you putting that comic book into the trash before I knock you into the middle of next week?"

I gulped. *Superman* was my favorite comic book. And I hadn't finished the story yet. But I didn't want to get myself into any further trouble, and I didn't feel like getting knocked into the middle of next week, so I walked over and dropped the issue into the wastepaper basket. I never did find out for certain how Superman was able to forestall the nuclear annihilation of Metropolis, but I know he did, because in the next issue Metropolis showed no signs of having been dropped into the ocean. But I'm getting ahead of myself.

Old Man McMahon stared into the wastebasket and said, "Good choice. Now what exactly did you imagine a printer's devil is supposed to do?"

"I've got no idea, sir. But whatever it is, I'm willing to do it for three hours a day, five days a week."

His face changed—I thought it could have been a smile, but I wasn't certain—and he said, "Follow me."

It turns out that a printer's devil is supposed to do all the jobs around a printing press that nobody else feels like doing—sweeping up, washing down equipment that has gotten too gummed up to function, stacking up huge rolls of paper once they've been delivered to the loading dock, scrubbing the toilets, replacing the toilet paper in the stalls, running to get coffee for Old Man McMahon and, last but certainly not least, watching the line. Watching the line was the most boring job of all, because all you were supposed to do was watch the colored pages come off the press and make sure they weren't ripped or folded over or anything. Virgil had been watching the line because Old Man McMahon's previous printer's devil had headed off to college. Now that I was on duty, I was the one who had to watch the line.

"It seems like about the most boring job in the world," Virgil said, "and maybe it is, because usually nothing goes wrong." I could hear him properly for the first time now. The press was shut down, and the plant was quiet enough. He was explaining to me what I was about to do. "But every once in a while, the sheets come off the press cockeyed and you can see them folding over on each other and getting all torn up. The second you see that, you need to hit the red button. That stops the press. The longer you wait to press that button, the more paper gets wasted and the bigger the chance the machine will be damaged. If you see *one* piece of paper come off the press off-kilter, you have to hit this big red button. No sleeping on the job. Got it?"

"Got it!"

I watched the line for 90 straight deadly dull minutes on my first day. Not one sheet of paper came off that rickety press in anything other than a perfect fashion. The machine was loud and huge, and the movements of its ancient works were creaky and repetitive. It was easily the most boring job I could imagine. The 90th minute of watching the line made me wish there were more toilets to clean. At least when I was cleaning toilets, I was *doing* something.

Day two: Old Man McMahon was back to scowling again. "You do know enough to push the big red button if anything goes wrong with the paper feed, don't you?"

I nodded.

"All right then. Don't screw that up. Here's a buck. Go get me a large coffee with extra cream and extra sugar. Bring me back the change. *All* the change. Then you'll watch the line."

I did as I was commanded. On the way back from the coffee shop, I saw that the new issue of *Superman* was out. Maybe when I got paid, I could buy it!

Having passed along the paper bag with the coffee (extra cream, extra sugar) and all of Old Man McMahon's change, I heard these hoarse words from the red, bald man who was my boss: "Time to watch the line. And don't you take your eye off those sheets, kid. Don't you dare. Or I'll knock you into the middle of next week."

That got my attention. I watched the line like a hawk for two hours and fifteen minutes. Nothing went wrong. I felt like my head was about to explode. When Virgil finally shut the press down, Old Man McMahon said, "Don't get cocky. You think nothing can happen? I'm telling you. Something can happen. And if you miss it, I'll knock you into the middle of next week."

Day three passed in much the same manner. So did days four and five. That brought me to the end of the week.

I got the weekend off, of course, and on Saturday morning my mom called me her "little man" and made me breakfast in bed. She told me she was proud of me and asked me which I preferred: working at McMahon's Press or going to school. I think she expected me to say the print shop. I had been pulling a D average during my last year of high school, and the guidance counselor had it in for me.

"School," I said, "hands down. School. At least you can do something at school. Most of the time I just watch the line at the press. That's not really doing anything. But it's payday on Monday. That means you can pay off that phone bill and we can get the phone turned back on. So I don't mind."

She looked at me like I was the heavyweight champion of the world or something, smiled a big smile as she poured me another glass of orange juice and put it on the tray, and called me her "little man" again. Then she said:

"When you get paid, you be sure to keep five dollars out of that fifty for yourself. You deserve that, Mickey. A working man needs a little walking-around money." And she smiled again and kissed me on the forehead.

I had the best mom in the world.

On day six, Old Man McMahon paid me with ten crumpled, sweaty five-dollar bills. Getting paid in real money made my chest puff out.

"Simpler to pay in cash," Old Man McMahon said. "Much less paperwork." I think he was dodging paying the taxes. Virgil got paid in cash, too. "Now here's another buck. You go out and get me a large coffee–"

"Extra cream, extra sugar," I said. "Got it."

"Don't interrupt your boss, kid," he growled. "And when you come back, it's time for you to watch the line. You keep an eagle eye out for twisted sheets coming off that press, or I'll have to knock you into the middle of next week. You hear me?"

"Yes, sir," I said.

On the way back from the coffee shop, I passed that same newsstand. The latest issue of *Superman* was still on display. This month, Superman was up against the robot monsters from Mars. I pulled one of the ragged five-dollar bills from my pocket for the newsstand guy—a tired-looking old man from what I guessed was China—and said, "Superman, please. That's my money, by the way. I earned that money. All by myself. I work at McMahon's Press."

The newsstand guy seemed unimpressed by this information. He just said, "Twenty cents," handed me my comic, and counted out my change.

I smiled anyway and stuffed the comic into the back waistband of my jeans, underneath my shirt so Virgil and Old Man McMahon would never spot it. I brought the coffee back to the shop. The minute I handed Old Man McMahon his coffee, Virgil started up the press, and McMahon shouted, over the rising noise: "Now, watch that line! Eagle eye, kid!"

I said, "Yes, sir." And I meant it. I really did.

My plan was to wait until I got home to read about Superman and the robot monsters from Mars. I swear it was. But this was a huge job. It was an advertising circular for the next week's Sunday paper, and there was a boring picture of broccoli on its front page. The time seemed to drag on forever. The clock on the wall told me that I watched the colored sheets roll off the press, into their bundles, and onto the assembly line that took them into the packing area for the warehouse crew for forty minutes. Then an hour. Then an hour and fifteen minutes. Then an hour and forty-five minutes. Then two hours and five minutes.

I swear, watching paint dry would have felt to me like watching the Super Bowl in person at that point. The machine creaked and wheezed and shuddered, again and again, and the colored circulars with the boring picture of broccoli on the front page kept on coming and coming. The print run simply refused to end.

At two hours and twenty-one minutes into the run, I had an idea. Surely taking one little glimpse at the very first page of the latest issue of *Superman* wouldn't do anyone any harm, would it?

The press was running fine. If it had gotten this far without anything misfeeding, surely I could sneak a peek for just a few seconds at the grand battle between the Man of Steel and the robot monsters from Mars.

The machine was positioned in such a way that Virgil couldn't see me, and Old Man McMahon was off somewhere meeting a client. Both of them were a little too intense about the whole "eagle eye" thing, anyway. Probably the machine had *never* misfed, and they were just being overcautious.

I pulled the comic book out of the back of my jeans, brought it around front, gazed again at the marvelous cover—Superman was about to deliver a ferocious blow to a steel-eyed red android—and took a deep breath.

I checked the line. It was fine—no misfeed.

I opened the comic book. Page one had a huge, colorful splash panel that showed a rocket taking off for the planet Mars. Reporters were busy jotting down notes, and photographers were taking pictures. One of the reporters was Lois Lane. She was thinking, "What a story!" as she scribbled furiously. Another of the reporters was Clark Kent. He was noticing something odd about the launch, and he was about to activate his X-ray vision to check out the possibility of sabotage within the structure of the rocket itself, when–

"Hey kid, I said to keep an eagle eye!"

The hoarse, shouting voice was Old Man McMahon's, and

his huge hand had just clapped hard onto the red button. The press moaned and groaned and shuddered to a halt. I looked over to the assembly line and saw a long, tangled pile of twisted, asymmetrical circulars, each torn and each fronted by a stalk of boring broccoli. It looked like all the stalks of broccoli were trying to eat each other alive.

Virgil stalked up and surveyed the damage. He mouthed a silent oath and shook his head darkly as he studied me. I felt Old Man McMahon's huge hand on my shoulder.

"My office," he said. "Right now."

The office was messy and smelled of coffee and cigarettes. I sat across from him, in the visitor's chair, and watched him glare at me from behind the desk. He seemed to be waiting for me to say something.

"I'm awfully sorry, Mr. McMahon, really I am-"

"Not yet, you're not. Not sorry enough. Get up and close that door before I knock you into the middle of next week. You hear me?"

I stood and did as he had told me to do, then returned to my seat. His face was red and huge, but his eyes were small and focused on the stupidest printer's devil in the universe: me.

"I swear I won't take my eye off the line again, Mr. McMahon. I swear it. Please don't fire me. My mom needs the money. Please let me keep the job. Please. My dad left us. My mom is counting on me to keep this money coming in. Please don't tell her about what I did. She'd have a horrible time with this."

At these words, his face softened, and I will never know exactly why. In the years since, I've told myself that he must have let his own mother down somehow, but I have no idea whether or not that's true. All I know is that the next thing he said to me was:

"You swear that's true, Mickey? That your mother's counting on this money?"

"Yes, sir. I swear it. On my soul, sir. Please don't tell her what happened. Please."

"Would Frankie back up that story, Mickey? That your mom needs this money? That your dad's not around anymore?"

"Sure he would, sir. You can ask him. Frankie knows my dad skipped town. Please don't fire me, Mr. McMahon. I won't do it again, sir. I swear. Please don't tell my mom what I did."

The big man with the bald scalp and the broad, sunburned face took a deep breath and stared up at the ceiling, then looked back down at me. He said, in a gentler tone than I had ever heard him use: "Listen, Mickey. This is a job. I know I yell at you a lot to get your attention. I yell at all the guys. That's how I work. I yell at people. But the person who really needs to get your attention now is you, Mickey. You can't count on me or on anybody else to make sure you do your job. Now that you have a job, you need to keep an eye on yourself. That's what a man does.

It's a serious thing. Now, you've got someone counting on you at home. I do, too. So does Virgil. So do each of the guys out in the plant. They've all got mouths to feed. That's serious business. That's responsibility. That's a job. You understand? A job. It's not a joke. It's serious business. Now, I'll let you keep this job if you can promise me you'll remember that it's your responsibility to get the job done, Mickey. Not anyone else's—yours. After all, you're not a kid anymore, Mickey. If you care about your mom— and I think you do—then you really mean what you say about never taking your eye off the line again. So I'll make you a deal. If you promise to do your job to the very best of your ability, and if you learn from this mistake, then I'll keep you on. If you ever make that mistake again, I'll let you go in a heartbeat. But if you can promise me you'll do your best, then yes, you can keep the job. And I won't tell your mom."

And he never did. I was grateful for that—and grateful, too, that he never knocked me into the middle of next week, though he still talked a lot about the possibility.

Maturity begins when one lives for others.

—**HERMANN HESSE**

CINDERELLA AND THE PLUGGER

"Do not be anxious about anything, but in every situation, by prayer and petition, with thanksgiving, present your requests to God."

—PHILIPPIANS 4:6

Many years ago, during what we now call the Great Depression, a man and woman living 500 miles apart discovered they had a mutual desire to improve their circumstances. That discovery was to change their lives forever, and the change only came about because of a dream.

Jack Kowalski was a young man in 1932. He was what was known then as a plugger. Pluggers worked hard. When things went badly for them, they found ways to put things right. If they were knocked down, they always found ways to get back up again, like a real champion always does. They did what was needed to make ends meet. They sold stuff, made stuff, or worked odd jobs.

Jack was raised on a tiny farm in Illinois. His parents were generous and caring, but if Jack and his older brother Henry had remained at home, there would have been no paid work for them to do—the town's breadlines were long—and no chance for them to improve their lives. When Henry was 18, he hit the road and was lucky enough, just a month or so later, to secure a job in a pottery factory in Johnstown, Pennsylvania. After that, there was a long stretch when he and Jack rarely saw each other in person. They communicated mainly by writing letters, as many people did during this period. The expression "Write when you find work" originated during this time. Millions of young men went out on their own like Henry did. Some of them found work, but most of them didn't. During the hardest years of the Great Depression, of which 1932 was definitely one, the official unemployment rate was 23.6%. If you figured in everyone who had stopped looking for a job, which was quite a few people, the unemployment rate was probably closer to 30%.

As soon as Jack was old enough, he left his home, just as his older brother had, and hit the road. Packing all his belongings into one small suitcase, he rode the rails in boxcars, stopping at various small towns and farming outposts along the way. When he arrived at a town, he would check his suitcase into a hotel safe. This cost far less than a room, allowing Jack to save money by sleeping in cornfields, haystacks, and barns.

He was only seventeen. He was strong and resilient. He didn't mind hearing "no" for an answer. He looked for odd jobs and sometimes found them—baling hay, repairing fences, and generally making himself useful to total strangers, most of whom were kind, some of whom fed him, and some of whom paid him *and* fed him. He worked hard everywhere he went, and by living so frugally, he was able to save almost every cent he earned. He had no permanent home. He figured it wasn't time for that yet.

He lived that way for two years.

* * * * *

In Johnstown, Henry had married a woman called Eleanor, whose childhood had been destroyed by a family tragedy. When Eleanor and her sister, Amy, were very young, their widowed mother, who had been remarried to a man named Theodore, had died. This left the two girls in the care of their grief-stricken and dispirited stepfather.

Theodore had not responded well to the loss of his wife. He had developed a drinking problem when his stepdaughters were very small, and the situation had not improved as the years passed. By the time Eleanor and Amy were teenagers, their stepfather seemed unable to seize any of the opportunities life gave him. His small farm produced less and less income, and he could find no employer willing to take him on. His frustration sometimes became so overwhelming that he lashed out at his two stepdaughters.

Eleanor and Amy kept house for their stepfather, cooking his meals and washing and mending his clothes. Eleanor had a job, but everything she earned went to caring for their stepfather, paying for minimal upkeep of the dilapidated home, and buying liquor.

Eleanor had been just nineteen years old when she met Henry Kowalski, who worked at the pottery factory where she had a job as a secretary. When the two passed each other in the vast hallway that led into the big rest area where workers ate their lunch, Eleanor noticed that Henry's eyes sparkled every time he glanced at her. She smiled back. He made a point of sitting next to her and chatting about his family's farm for four straight days, even though men weren't supposed to sit at the women's dining table. The foreman made him move on the fifth day. On the sixth day, when he asked Eleanor to marry him, just outside the factory gates, she agreed enthusiastically.

After Eleanor's departure, her younger sister Amy was left alone to care for her stepfather. The money was even tighter now, so he made her take a job in the pottery factory, where she worked long hours while he sat at home and drank too much. When Amy came home, she was still expected to do all the cooking, cleaning, and washing. As the only child left in the house, she took the brunt of her stepfather's angry, drunken rants. Somehow, through it all, she found a way to smile. Like a modern-day Cinderella, she dreamed of leaving her difficult life for something better. She knew her moment would come. She prayed that God would hasten that moment.

* * * * *

Time passed. Eleanor often discussed her sister's plight with her new husband. She knew, deep in her heart, that she had been right to accept Henry's proposal, but she still felt guilty for having left Amy.

For his part, Henry thought every day about his brother and his rootless existence. Henry loved married life. He relished the companionship and the sense of purpose that came with having a wife.

Eleanor had recently given birth to their first child, a boy. One evening, as the small family sat by the fireplace after a busy day, Henry had an idea. As he gazed with deep love at his wife and the fragile bundle she held in her arms, he thought that this was exactly the kind of life Jack needed to settle him down.

"What if Jack and Amy got married?" he said.

Eleanor's face glowed. She said she thought this was a wonderful idea—if they liked each other.

So Henry wrote a long letter to Jack and told him all about Amy. He told him about her patience, her smile, and her trials in the abusive household she lived in. He extolled the benefits of married life. He sent the letter to the last address he had for his brother, which was in Gary, Indiana. Unfortunately, he forgot to put a stamp on the letter.

The letter came back marked "insufficient postage" while Henry was at work. Eleanor, busy caring for the baby, set it aside without realizing what it was. A month or so later, Henry got a letter from Jack that didn't mention anything about Eleanor's sister, and he assumed his brother had quietly dismissed the idea of marriage. He resolved not to mention it again.

Then the miracle happened.

Henry had a terrifying dream in which his brother Jack had missed a train, and as a result, thanks to the dark logic of nightmares, the two brothers had been separated forever. In the dream, Jack somehow told Henry, from across the world, "You should have mailed me about it."

"I did," Henry said in the dream. "I swear I did."

But his brother only repeated, "You should have mailed me about it," and then he started to vanish.

Henry woke in a cold sweat, rose from his bed without waking his wife, and went, for reasons he could never explain, to the kitchen table. There, in a pile of papers he found stacked beneath a book his wife had been reading, he found the letter marked "insufficient postage."

Henry grabbed a pen and a piece of paper. He sat down and started writing.

* * * * *

Jack received the new letter Henry wrote about the missing stamp, the nightmare, and the possibility of matrimony just as he was about to begin a long railway journey out of St. Louis, where he had been staying in a boarding house he didn't much like because the people there always looked at him funny when he talked about opening a grocery store. He read his brother's letter in an open railway carriage, with a cold wind freezing his feet. He had grown used to riding the rails—maybe too used to it. He stared out through the widely spaced metal slats of the freight car and thought long and hard about Henry's suggestion.

For Jack, marriage was not a new idea. He had always viewed it as something that should be taken very seriously. He now had quite a lot of money saved in hopes of opening a store and getting married. For two years now, he had put aside every penny he could, determined to be ready when the right time and the right girl came along. He'd never found her. He wondered, though, if this might be her.

By the end of the train journey, Jack had decided to move forward. He got off at DeKalb, Illinois, the town whose property values he had been studying at the St. Louis Public Library, and wrote back to Henry, saying that he was interested in courting Eleanor's sister.

*   *   *   *   *

And so it was that Jack and Amy's courtship came about courtesy of the US Postal Service. It would also be carried out through the mail.

Jack tapped his savings, bought a house in DeKalb, and began to set up the little grocery store he had been planning for so long. The foreclosed property he'd found was perfect. It had a storefront right beneath the living quarters. In the meantime, he wrote letters to Amy, waited for her letters to come, and read and reread what she wrote.

From the very start, Jack and Amy felt a powerful connection. For six months they discussed the details of their lives by mail, and with each exchange of letters they felt a warmth grow between them. Jack wrote about his life on the road and about his plans for a prosperous future. He told her about the work he was doing to get the store ready. Amy wrote about the difficulties of her life with her stepfather and about her dreams of leaving. She shared her fond memories of her mother and sister with Jack. Although her circumstances were painful, she always seemed to find a way to look on the bright side. Jack often felt that he could see her smiling when he read her letters.

Eventually, Jack decided that the time had come to act. It's hard to imagine such a thing today, in our era of instant photographs and text messaging, but without hearing her voice or seeing a single photograph of her, the Plugger popped the question to Cinderella—in writing. It was the shortest letter he had ever sent her.

It said: "Amy, I believe we should be married. Are you agreeable to this? I promise always to treasure you deeply. Yours very truly, Jack Kowalski."

The day that Amy's response came in the mail, Jack's heart was in his mouth. His fingers trembled as he opened the envelope. But he need not have worried. Amy had written a cautious acceptance.

"Visit me," she wrote. "Come here and spend one day in my company. If at the end of the day, we both still feel that it's a good idea, we should go ahead and get married."

Such was the power of their pen-and-paper courtship that Jack did not hesitate for a moment. Having made the necessary arrangements, he climbed into his well-used Chevy Coupe and drove the bone-rattling 500 miles to Johnstown, Pennsylvania, to spend a day with Amy. When he finally saw her, he felt a joy he had never known before. Her face reflected the warmth of his own feelings. Chaperoned by Henry and Eleanor, Amy and Jack spent a joyous day together exploring Johnstown in Jack's Chevy. When evening came—and it came quickly—the two asked for some time alone, and Henry and Eleanor retired. On the front porch of his brother's home, Jack took her hand and made the proposal out loud that had previously been made only on paper. He used the same words.

"Yes!" responded Amy, beaming.

It was agreed that Jack would drive back a month later to pick up his bride. But now, Jack had a long drive back to Illinois. It was the happiest day of his life. He felt peaceful as he thought of the days that lay ahead—and of the hard work, perseverance, and cautious planning that had gone into making them possible.

* * * * *

Only one person was not happy to hear of this match: Amy's stepfather, Theodore, was disgusted when he realized that he was soon to lose his live-in servant. At first, he spoke kindly to her, trying to convince her that he loved her and wanted her to stay. When this did not change her mind, he became angry. The evenings became impossible.

After serving him dinner, Amy avoided Theodore. They ate in silence, and then she went to her room, locked the door, and listened to music and baseball games on the radio. Her heart was so full of love for Jack that the days and nights of that long, difficult month passed more easily.

One night, as Amy was getting ready to serve dinner, Theodore cornered her in the kitchen. He had obviously had too much to drink. After shouting out a stream of increasingly bitter words—all of them words that Amy wished she had never heard and would never hear again—he raised his hand as if to hit her, something he had never done before.

In her fear and confusion, Amy pushed him aside, fled to her room, and locked the door.

* * * * *

On the day Jack finally arrived at Amy's home in the same Chevy Coupe he had traveled in a month earlier, Amy climbed into the car and waved goodbye to the difficult life she had known. In truth, she was waving goodbye to the house where she had lived with her mother and sister, not to the vicious man within it. Theodore refused to come out most days, and this was one of those days.

On the way to DeKalb, the couple made only one stop, in Toledo. There they found a Justice of the Peace who performed the marriage ceremony. Amy insisted that they tie the knot before they spend the night under the same roof together.

A Bible passage that characterizes Amy's life—the kind of person she was, and the kinds of actions that resulted—is Proverbs 31:10-31. It reads as follows:

> A wife of noble character who can find? She is worth far more than rubies. Her husband has full confidence in her and lacks nothing of value. She brings him good, not harm, all the days of her life.
>
> She selects wool and flax and works with eager hands. She is like the merchant ships, bringing her food from afar. She gets up while it is still night; she provides food for her family and portions for her female servants. She considers a field and buys it; out of her earnings she plants a vineyard. She sets about her work vigorously; her arms are strong for her tasks. She sees that her trading is profitable, and her lamp does not go out at night. In her hand she holds the distaff and grasps the spindle with her fingers.
>
> She opens her arms to the poor and extends her hands to the needy.

When it snows, she has no fear for her household; for all of them are clothed in scarlet. She makes coverings for her bed; she is clothed in fine linen and purple.

Her husband is respected at the city gate, where he takes his seat among the elders of the land.

She makes linen garments and sells them, and supplies the merchants with sashes.

She is clothed with strength and dignity; she can laugh at the days to come. She speaks with wisdom, and faithful instruction is on her tongue.

She watches over the affairs of her household and does not eat the bread of idleness.

Her children arise and call her blessed; her husband also, and he praises her: "Many women do noble things, but you surpass them all." Charm is deceptive, and beauty is fleeting; but a woman who fears the Lord is to be praised. Honor her for all that her hands have done, and let her works bring her praise at the city gate.

Jack and Amy had a very happy and grateful marriage—one that lasted 56 years. They had five children, started a business that outlasted one Great Depression and five recessions, and had the time of their lives. All of their children and all their friends said that theirs was a match made in heaven, and neither of them ever disputed that. Of course, things weren't always easy, but Jack kept his promise and deeply treasured Amy, who always found a way to smile and support her husband—and to be very grateful.

"Success in marriage does not come merely through finding the right mate, but through being the right mate."

—BARNETT BRICKNER

HELEN'S STORY*

"Is prayer your steering wheel or your spare tire?"

—CORRIE TEN BOOM

In 1943, my father received an offer of a job in Austria. He
was to work the land on a small farm, which belonged to a
prosperous farmer. My family—my mother and father, my two

---

brothers, Tony and Al, and I—were all glad to make the move. The farm was in a beautiful location, beside woods and a small creek. It was close to the border with Yugoslavia, where we came from, and we would be able to visit our relatives easily.

There was a motto in my family: "If you are old enough to walk, you are old enough to work." We all worked hard. Along with his farming duties, my father worked as a lumberjack. As a result, he was often away from home, and it was left to my "Pioneer Mom" to manage things at home. We all had chores. We had to feed the animals, fetch water from the well, pull weeds, and help Mom in the fields. When I think back on those times, I can still picture Mom in the fields, her face burned red by the sun, her hair held back with a scarf. I can picture myself as a small child, running alongside her, helping with the planting.

When we finished a day's work in the fields, Mom and I would go home, where there was even more work waiting for us. We did the laundry, and we cooked and cleaned. When my brothers got home from school, they would clean the barn and feed the animals.

Although we all worked very hard, I remember those days as happy times. Our house was small, and one of the rooms was rented out to a woman named Mrs. Sehlinger and her granddaughter. They were nice neighbors.

My brothers and I loved exploring. We spent what little free time we had running around the farm, playing hide and seek in the hay sheds, and wading in the creek, where we could watch the tiny fish fluttering about in the water, too fast and too tiny for us to catch.

Things changed when the soldiers came.

Al and I were splashing in the creek one day. Tony was standing on the bank, getting ready to jump in, when he spotted something nearby. "Al! Helen! Look. There's a soldier," he called. We climbed out of the creek and looked in the direction where he was pointing. There were two soldiers, both wearing grey uniforms, long rifles propped up against their shoulders.

Quickly, we dried off and ran back to the house. When we told Mom about the soldiers, she said, "Keep away from the creek. There is no reason for you to be down there."

I was sad about this. It was a hot summer, and it was fun to splash in the waters. But later, Dad told us that the creek was right beside the border between Austria and Yugoslavia. "We can't go there anymore," he said.

"But what about when we are visiting our relatives?" I asked.

"No," he replied. "We can't do that anymore. It is forbidden."

One evening, while my father was away from home, we were eating our supper and there was a loud knock at the door. Mom answered. It was three of the soldiers. They seemed very large in our small kitchen, with their tall black boots and their guns.

"Get away from the table," one of them said, waving his gun.

Frightened, we moved away quickly. The soldiers sat down in our seats and started to eat the bread and stew we were having for supper. My brothers and I were horrified, but Mom gestured at us to be quiet. "Do your homework," she whispered to my brothers. They took out their books and began to work quietly on the bench in the corner.

When the soldiers had finished eating our food, they sat back in their chairs. One of them threw off his boots and stretched out his feet. Another began to smoke a cigar. After a while, one of them said to my brothers, "What are you doing?"

"Our homework," Tony answered.

"Let me see," said the soldier.

The other soldiers laughed. Tony handed over his books, and the soldier started to look through them.

One of the books was a religious book, and when the soldier found it, he stood up, flicking through the pages. Then he leaned his face down toward my brothers. "You realize, I hope, that there is no god," he proclaimed.

None of us said anything. We were so scared.

"There is no god," the soldier repeated. "Only Hitler. Hitler is our god." He threw the books onto the ground, and the soldiers left.

After they were gone, Mom reached out and hugged us all, but she was shivering. I could tell she was scared too.

For a while, the soldiers left us in peace and life was good again. But soon they began to visit a lot. Some of them were polite or decent, but many were rude and mean. They came at all times of the day and night, sometimes looking for information, sometimes for food. Whatever they wanted, they took. They had guns, and there was nothing we could do.

There would be a knock at the door. "Is Herr Knap at home?" (That was how they referred to my father.)

"No."

"When will he be home?"

"I don't know."

"We will wait."

One day, they arrived before school was finished. Only Mom and I were at home.

"Where is Herr Knap?"

"He's not at home."

"We will search for him."

They went all around the house, looking for my father. Then they went into the barn where we kept the hay. After a few minutes, one of them shouted for Mom and me to join them there.

"What is that?" asked one of the soldiers.

He was pointing at a small, hollowed-out cave in among the haystacks. This was one of the places my brothers and I liked to hide when we were playing. I explained this. The soldier frowned. "Where are your brothers?" he asked.

When my mother explained that my brothers were at school, the soldiers decided to wait for them to come back. As soon as Tony and Al arrived, the soldiers led them into the barn and interrogated them.

"What are they doing?" I asked Mom.

"They are trying to see whether your brothers will say the same thing you did," Mom answered.

"Will they arrest us?" I asked.

"No," she said, and she hugged me close. When the soldiers came out of the barn, bringing my brothers back to us, one of them said, "If anyone comes asking you to hide them, you must report them."

"Yes, we will," my mother said.

"Heil Hitler," said the soldier, and they left. My mother made no response.

Sundays were a day of rest in our family. Mom would cook dinner, and after we ate, she would tell us stories. Sometimes, these stories were from the Bible. Other times, she made them up. I still remember some of the stories my Mom told us during that time.

One Sunday, while Mom was telling us a story, there was a sharp knocking at the door.

My father was in the room at the time. He and Mom exchanged frightened glances.

"Go out of the back door," she said.

He went, and she answered the door, where she once again found three soldiers.

"Is Herr Knap at home?"

"No."

"Where is he?"

"I don't know."

"We will search for him," they said again.

They looked in all the rooms and then went out into the yard. While the soldiers had been looking through the house, my father had gone into the barn and hidden deep in the hay. In the house, we sat quietly in the kitchen and waited, terrified.

"We should pray," Mom said. All of us held hands and bowed our heads. I prayed, over and over again, that the soldiers would not find my father. I could tell that Mom and my brothers were praying for the same thing.

Eventually, the soldiers came back to the house. "We will come again," one of them said. Then they left.

As soon as it seemed safe to do so, we went looking for my father. We called his name until he came.

When Dad came out, covered in strands of hay, he said that the soldiers had looked for him in the haystack. He said that they took pitchforks and thrust them deep into the hay. He said that one of the forks reached him, and pierced his side, just a little. He showed us the mark on his skin where it had grazed him.

To this day, I have believed that it was our prayers that saved Dad that evening.

A few days later, the soldiers came again, still looking for my father. Mom said, "He isn't home."

One of the soldiers took his gun and pointed the barrel at the pot of stew on the oven. "Why are you cooking for him?" he said. "When we see him, we will shoot him. We have orders to do so."

Standing beside her, I could feel Mom trembling, but as she spoke, she stayed very calm. "Well, if you are going to shoot him," she said, "you might as well just shoot all of us." I thought to myself, *Speak for yourself, Mom.*

The soldier smiled a thin, horrible smile. "That can be arranged," he said. "We're going next door to visit Frau Sehlinger. We'll be back."

While the soldiers were talking to Frau Sehlinger, Mom gathered all of us together and we went out the side door. We ran across the yard, Mom carrying my baby sister Frances and Al carrying my brother Frankie. We got to the woods and began walking through the trees. There were soldiers sitting just under the trees.

"Where are you going?" one of them called.

"To the doctor," Mom called back.

Once we were out of sight of the soldiers, we ran. For two weeks, we stayed with friends in town, not knowing if Dad was dead or alive. Every night that we were in town, we would pray together for God to keep Dad safe.

When we returned to our house, we were surprised and overjoyed to find Dad there, sitting at the kitchen table. We all started crying with happiness and relief. Dad explained that he had seen the soldiers coming and hid in the woodshed beside the house. When they went to look in the barn again, he slipped back into the house and hid in the large oven Mom used to bake bread. He stayed there for hours, until he was sure that the soldiers were gone. After that, whenever he heard the soldiers coming, he would climb into the oven once again.

Talk about a cat with nine lives!

That night, Mom and Dad sat us all down in the kitchen and explained that we had to find a way to leave, to get to a better place. Dad said that he had spoken to a friend and arranged to get us papers that would allow us to leave the country. As a family, we all prayed that we would escape to somewhere safe.

The first boat we could have booked passage on would have taken us to Argentina. But Mom didn't pass the physical. So we ended up getting on the next boat, which for some reason didn't require a doctor's exam. This boat was bound for America. Frau Sehlinger told us that in America, oranges grow in your back-yard and the floor shines like a mirror. (Later we learned that you had to live in Florida to grow oranges and that you had to scrub and wax the floors to make them shine! But at the time, her words sounded amazing to us.)

That night, we all took a moment to pray as a family for safe transit to America.

Weeks later, our ship pulled into New York. Before we arrived, Mom gathered us together one more time and we said a prayer of hope for our new life.

When we went out onto the decks, we could see the Statue of Liberty. What a beautiful sight that was. Around us, everyone was crying and shouting "America! America!" It was a wonderful sound.

"We are free," Mom said, smiling and hugging us, "free and safe at last." She was crying, and no more words came out for a while. But I was thinking, *This is what an answered prayer feels like.* And I was never more grateful for anything in my life.

"If the only prayer you said was thank you, that would be enough."

—MEISTER ECKHART

THE TAILOR'S MAGIC COAT

"Happiness is only real when shared."

—JON KRAKAUER

When I was growing up, my father spoke little about his home country of Slovenia. He was a quiet man most of the time, but whenever I asked about his past, he would clam up entirely.

It may have been that the memories were too painful. After

125

all, my father had left his family and traveled thousands of miles away from everything and everyone he had ever known. Travel was different then. These days, we can contact friends on the other side of the world in the blink of an eye. Back then, letters took weeks to arrive. Air travel was not a possibility, except for a few very wealthy and brave souls. Traveling from Europe to America meant a weeks-long boat journey.

When my father left Slovenia, it must have seemed almost like traveling to another planet. He would not have expected to see his family again. I cannot imagine how he must have missed them.

Growing up, I found myself fascinated by the fact that I had grandparents who lived thousands of miles away and did not speak a word of English. Even if we met, we would not have understood each other. And if I wrote them a letter, they would not have been able to read it.

"They can't read," said my mother when I questioned her, frustrated at my dad's lack of answers. "Not very well, anyway."

"So, what does Dad write, when he writes to them?" I asked.

"He keep the words simple," she said, "and sometimes he sends them little pictures you and your brothers and sisters draw. His mother loves those. She puts them on her wall."

"Did he send my picture of the train engine?" I asked. I was very proud of that picture. As I stood near the engine, the smoke rose from the chimney and went curling into the sky.

"Yes, he sent the picture of the train engine," my mom replied.

It was strange to imagine my picture on the wall of a farmyard kitchen thousands of miles away. I liked to imagine the farm in Slovenia. My mother said it was a very beautiful country, full of green fields, thick forests, and mountains. But my mother had never seen Slovenia. She was just telling me what she had heard.

When I asked my father about Slovenia, he only grunted and said, "I have to keep working. This coat will not sew itself."

My father was a tailor. He produced clothes of such high quality that men would travel as far as 100 miles to buy them.

Now among the vast array of suits, jackets, ties, shirts, and other items that my father worked on for his clients was a green coat. I first saw this coat on a dark winter's evening, laid out on my father's work table, its mother-of-pearl buttons gleaming.

"Who's that for?" I asked.

"A very special client," he answered.

But the weeks went by, and no one ever came to the store to collect the coat. My father kept working on it. It was made of a beautiful, soft fabric that glistened in the lamplight, and every stitch was sewn to perfection. I decided that it must be for someone very rich, and I wondered why they never called to ask why it was taking so long.

For months, my father worked on the jacket, but then one day, it was gone from his worktable. I looked in the store, but there was no sign of it on any of the shelves or hangers.

"What happened to the coat?" I asked my father.

"What coat?"

"The green one ... with the buttons."

He grunted and said something inaudible, turning to continue his work. I understood that he did not want to tell me. It was strange.

Years passed, and I forgot all about the coat. Eventually, I left home to go to school. After that, I was so busy that I rarely visited my parents. When I received a phone call telling me that my father had died, I felt a deep sadness at all the time I had spent away from home, all the hours I could have been near him but wasn't. After the funeral, I went home with my mother. The house that had once seemed so full and welcoming now seemed empty and cold. The day was overcast, and the sky was dark grey at mid-morning.

"What will you do?" I asked my mother.

She looked around at the walls, lined with framed photos that held five decades of memories of our family. "I can't stay here right now," she said, her voice low and sad. "Maybe in a little while ... maybe not. I haven't decided. But for the moment, I will go and stay with my sister."

While my mother was away, I took it on myself to keep an eye on the house. I would visit once a week, lighting the lamps and kindling a fire in the fireplace, making sure that the house did not lose that feeling of having been lived in. I walked from room to room, remembering happy times from when I was a child.

One frigid, grey day, in my father's shop, I noticed a small cupboard door, built into the attic eave, which I had never noticed before. I decided to see what was in it. With a chair to stand on, I pulled at the door handle, but it had wedged shut with time. I pulled harder, and eventually I got the door open.

Inside the door, on a hanger, was the green coat.

I recognized it immediately, for it had been part of my life for many months. I took the green coat out of the cupboard, noticing as I did so how well-cared-for it seemed. Any other piece of clothing left in a cupboard for years would have grown worn and musty and moth-eaten. But the green coat's material shone like new, and its mother-of-pearl buttons gleamed as if they had been polished that very day.

When I examined the coat, I discovered a folded-up piece of paper in one of the pockets. The paper had yellowed slightly with age, and it crackled as I unfolded it.

It was a note, in my father's writing. It said: "Dear Erik, I made this coat for you, so that you can see what I saw. Wear it, and you will know about our history."

The letter seemed to make no sense. *It's just a coat,* I thought. *What can he mean?*

Nonetheless, something told me to put it on, and I felt strangely happy as I did so. It was light and warm and every bit as comfortable as I had imagined. I fastened the buttons, and the coat was snug on my body. It fit perfectly!

I heard the sound of children laughing from the direction of the kitchen.

"Who's there?" I called. The house was supposed to be empty. The voices trailed away.

Although I wanted to make my way to the kitchen to investigate, a sudden, inexplicable urge to sleep came over me.

I followed my feet as they led me, of their own accord, into my old bedroom, where I collapsed on the bed instantly and fell under the spell of what must have been the deepest slumber of my life. I wasn't sure, but I thought I heard the sounds of children laughing and singing.

I dreamed that my father sat across from my bed. I was a little boy again, watching him sew and sew and sew. Every time I tried to get him to speak to me, he only looked at me and smiled— this stood out because he was a man who rarely smiled—and then held up the green coat he was working on. Then he looked back down and resumed his work.

I woke to a clinking of pots and pans in the kitchen, as well as the smell of eggs and farm-rich bacon. I heard the sounds of muffled voices coming from that part of the house, and I thought, *Am I still dreaming?*

I heard dogs barking outside, cows mooing from not so far away, and a rooster crowing. Somehow it seemed to have gotten lighter outside.

Still wearing the finely-tailored green coat, I found my way to the open kitchen, where I had heard the voices and laughter of children. There I found a middle-aged woman in an apron. She was quite beautiful, and she looked strangely familiar to me. She looked out a window and said something in another language that I didn't understand. Then, she went back to her cooking.

"Hello," I said, but she didn't appear to hear me.

I looked around, and, feeling increasingly uncertain of my surroundings, meandered back to the room where I had awoken and closed the door behind me. The place seemed different somehow. It took me a few moments, but then I realized that the walls around me had changed. They were just planks of wood, without plaster or paint. The wardrobe had vanished. There was no bed—only a large table and rows of shelves full of bags of food: flour, grains, and seeds of some kind.

The door to the room opened and two children, a girl and a boy, came running in. They did not see me. Chattering in a language I did not understand but that somehow seemed familiar, they flung themselves under one of the shelves. The girl pressed her finger to her lips, and they both became quiet. Soon after this, another boy came into the room. He was a little taller than the others, and I felt sure that I recognized his face from somewhere. After a while, I realized that he looked just like a photograph my mother had on her mantelpiece—a photograph of me.

The boy crept around the room and then went to the door. He was about to walk out, but then he turned and plunged toward the shelf where the other children were hiding. I couldn't make out what he said to them, but I expect it was something like "Found you!"

A woman's voice called from another room. Giggling, the children went out. I followed. Now, I found myself in a farm kitchen. There was a large wooden table in the middle of the room and an old wood-burning stove in one corner. The woman I had tried to speak to earlier was sitting at the table. She wore a bright-colored shawl over her head and shoulders. She smiled at the children as they came in but seemed to look right through me. Apparently, no one could see me.

One of the children opened a door close to the table, and a rush of warm air and bright sunlight came through. He was calling through the door, possibly to his father, and I took the chance to step outside.

I found myself in a small yard. To one side of me was a row of wooden sheds. The squawk of some kind of fowl could be heard through gaps in the walls. In front of me was a lush, green field filled with grapevines. Beyond that was a bank of pine trees, which stretched upward into snow-capped mountains beyond. It was incredibly beautiful. The air was warm and rich with the scent of pine.

A well-built young man came from one of the sheds. He was wearing old workman's clothes and a cap. Only when he passed me on his way into the house did I realize whom he resembled: my grandfather. (I had seen plenty of photos of him, but they were all from when he was much older.)

It was then that I remembered the note my father had written to me and realized what had happened. This was the house my father grew up in.

He was not a talkative man, but he was a skilled tailor. Instead of telling me about the world where he had grown up, he had used his skills to show me—and had somehow taken me back in time.

For the next hour, I wandered around my grandparents' world, watching the family as they ate their dinner, viewing the children as they helped with chores on the farm and then played in the large hay barn behind the house. I watched my grandmother as she cleaned up after dinner and then sat in the corner of the kitchen, sewing in the light of the fire. She had a beautiful, loving face, and I imagined her as she must have looked years later, in this same kitchen, as she sat in this very spot looking at a painting on the wall—one that had been painted thousands of miles away by a grandson she would never meet.

When evening came, and the family went to bed, I stood and watched the sun set beyond the beautiful Slovenian mountains, thinking about my father and how he had made up for years of silence with this unique and magical gift.

When the sun had finally set, I reached down and began to unbutton the coat. The instant I undid the first button, I saw my father. I was back in my bedroom, where I found that I was a little boy again, and my father was sitting across from me. A pleading expression was in his eyes.

"The coat is finished," he said. "You've seen what you asked about for yourself. You've seen your family. You've seen our homeland—and our home. And now, I have something to ask of you. Before you take the coat off, promise me you will tell your mother that I hope she will visit here soon. This was her home. She belongs here. She can be happy here again. Promise me you will tell her that."

I nodded and said, "I promise."

When I woke, it was still daytime. The clouds were gone, and the sun was pouring in through the window. The house that had seemed so cold suddenly felt warm and welcoming. I was still wearing the lovely green coat—but I noticed that the top button was undone.

I picked up the phone and called my mother. She had been hoping to talk to me, and the first thing she said was, "I just had the strangest dream about your father." I smiled knowingly, sure that I knew exactly what she had dreamed, and we were both very grateful.

Love is that condition in which the happiness
of another person is essential to your own.

—Robert A. Heinlein

THE DUKES OF THE RAILS

"We sinned for no reason but an incomprehensible lack of love, and He saved us for no reason but an incomprehensible excess of love."

—PETER KREEFT

The older man, who sat in the corner and wheezed with every breath, was the first to speak. He had been watching the younger man for a long time.

"Never expected to see a green kid like you jumpin' onto a movin' boxcar in the middle of the night. No, sir. Daytime, maybe. Not after midnight. No, sir. Not safe for kids to ride so late."

"I'm not a kid. I'm twenty-one. I've got a right to be here."

"Railroad president might not think so."

"I don't suppose he'd think either of us has a right to be here. But here we are. Anyway he's not around to complain now, is he?"

"No, sir. You're right there. But if you don't mind my sayin' so, you're awful young to be out ridin' the rails after midnight. Aren't you?"

"Am I?"

"Yes, sir. Way too young. Wouldn't pick you as twenty-one. You're not cut out for that kind of life. Late-night jumpers are a rough bunch. You don't want to run into one of those fellas at the end of the line. They're mean."

"It ain't like you got a first-class ticket in your pocket."

"I just don't like to see kids ridin' the rails when they don't have to is all. No, sir, I don't."

"Who says I don't have to? And why do you keep callin' me 'sir'?"

There was a pause as the older man negotiated a ragged, labored cough. After the convulsion passed, he said:

"By any chance you runnin' away from something bad, kid?"

"That's none of your business. And don't call me kid, either."

"Well, you might say please!"

"Please, then. Please don't call me kid."

"Okay. I won't call you that. I promise. No, I won't. Now I'm a man of my word. I won't call you kid, and I won't call you sir. So what am I goin' to call you instead? Well?"

"You can call me Jack."

"All right. Is that your name?"

"Guess it is now."

"Fair enough. Jack, are you really twenty-one?"

"Of course I am. I said I was twenty-one, didn't I?"

"Have to tell you, you come off a lot younger than that."

"Can't much help how I look, can I? If I said my name is Jack, it's Jack. If I said I'm twenty-one, I'm twenty-one. That's how it is now. Things are as I say they are."

The old man wheezed, stood, leaned forward, took a few long, strained breaths, straightened himself, studied his companion, and then lowered himself back down into his corner again with due care. He settled himself behind a dirty knapsack and what might have been a bag of potatoes.

"Right. Well, you've got me convinced. Your name is Jack, and you're twenty-one years of age. That means you're legal, though it doesn't mean you can't get in trouble with the railroad, and it doesn't mean you can't get in trouble at the end of the line. Now, you got on in Decatur. I wonder if you might happen to have some family in Decatur?"

"Not anymore."

"Jack, can I speak plainly to you?"

"Say whatever you want to say. I can't do much to stop you, can I?"

The older man wheezed after every sentence as he said:

"There's a lotta bad people who ride the rails. Lotta people who'll try to take advantage of a young person. They're out there. I know they are. Now, I happen to be a Christian man. Don't ask me how I got to be ridin' the rails at my age, because it's too long a story, and it's not worth tellin' anyway. But I'm a Christian man, whether I'm ridin' the rails or eatin' lobster thermidor, and I've done both. And I do look for ways to serve my Lord and maker, and I do make a point of takin' care of the young people who ride the rails and find themselves without any place to go. There are ways for me to serve the Lord, and that is one of those ways to serve. I've helped a lotta young people get off the rails, Jack—and get themselves into a better place."

The older man delivered another long, low, moaning cough. It took a while for that to finish up. Then he said, "Do you believe what I'm sayin' to you, Jack?"

"I guess I don't have any reason why I *shouldn't* believe you.

140

But it's all the same to me whether you tell the truth or lie to me about ridin' the rails or bein' a Christian or helpin' kids. It don't matter much to me. I ain't goin' back to Decatur."

"I wouldn't ever make you go there if that's not what you want to do, Jack. I promise. I won't ever try. But I can't believe you want to be here in a boxcar any longer than you absolutely have to be. If you let me, I will help you get off the rails and into a better place."

"Oh yeah? Why would you do that?"

"I'll do that because I want to get on God's good side, Jack."

Jack laughed. It was a cold laugh, harsher to the old man's ear than he liked to hear from a young person.

"You headed out to visit your maker tonight, do you think?" Jack laughed at his own joke, even louder than he'd laughed before, but when he noticed that the older man wasn't even smiling, he stopped laughing. "Well, are you?"

"Don't like to say. But I need a promise from you if I'm goin' to help you."

"What's that?"

"I need you to tell me the truth."

"Do you now?"

"If you don't tell me the truth tonight, then I can't do a thing for you. But if you tell me the truth, we can do business, and I can protect you from some of the rough characters who ride these rails at night and who know how to make things even worse for you than they are now. They're waitin' for you at the end of the line."

"What kinda rough characters? What would they be likely to do?"

The older man told him.

Jack said, "You promise you won't try to send me back to Decatur?"

"Not unless you ask me to. If you don't ask, then no, I won't. I swear on my Lord and Savior Jesus Christ that I won't ever try to send you back to Decatur, Jack—or even suggest that you go back. If you've got a reason for leavin', I'll have to respect that. You get to make your own choices, now don't you?"

"I don't have a home in Decatur. Not goin' to pretend I do any longer."

"I can tell."

The old man let out another long, raw cough. It lasted even longer than the others had.

The younger man said, "Nope. Not goin' back to Decatur. My old man beat me one too many times. That's the truth. One too many times. Not goin' back there. I'm goin' to live out on the road. Lotta people do it."

"All right then. That's your choice. You're a man now, I suppose, and you gotta right to make your own way."

The clickety-clack of the rails sounded above the silence. Finally the younger man said:

"You don't look too good. You would tell me if you needed a doctor or somethin', wouldn't you?"

"Don't like to say, and it doesn't much matter, because the smart man will always operate on the assumption that tonight's the night. The smart man always tries to get in one more good deed for the day, on the theory that the next mornin' can't be taken for granted. You goin' to help me do my one more good deed, Jack? You goin' to tell me the truth tonight? Well?"

"My name's not Jack. It's Sidney. I'm fifteen years old."

"It's a pleasure to meet you, Sidney."

"I won't swear on Jesus or anything. But yes, I'll tell you the truth—if you promise not to send me back to Decatur or help anyone else do that. You're not plannin' on dyin' in this boxcar tonight, are you, mister?"

"Sidney, you don't have to call me 'mister.' Call me Pat. It's the name my mother gave me the day I first saw her, and nobody's come up with a better one since. Will you call me that, Sidney? Instead of 'mister'?"

"You didn't answer my question, Pat."

"Well. Who says my plans matter? What matters is, we're tellin' each other the truth now. So, you're broke, aren't you? Or close to it? Remember: You told me you'd give me the truth."

"Not quite broke."

"How close?"

"I saved up nine dollars and forty-eight cents before I left town. I'm not stupid, you know. I didn't walk out of the house with nothin'. I knew I'd need some money if I was goin' to live out on the road. I worked at the hardware store for nearly three months. I saved up everything I could."

"Nine dollars and forty-eight cents."

"Yes. I told you I'm not stupid. I didn't leave that house with no money in my pocket. I'm goin' to live on the road now. I'm a planner. I plan ahead."

"Well, I'm glad to hear it, Sidney. A planner is a good thing to be when there's a depression on. Where do you suppose you'll get off?"

"Don't know yet."

"Got any friends? Got any family who'll take you in?"

"No and no. All I know is I promised myself I wasn't goin' to spend one more night in that house. I've got my nine dollars and forty-eight cents. I'll be all right."

"Well, that nine forty-eight will last you a little while—but maybe less time than you think. Any idea what you're goin' to do for work?"

"Don't know yet. Dig ditches, maybe. My dad always says it's the only thing I'm good for. Only thing I'll ever be good for, diggin' ditches. Sometimes when he gets sore at me he wallops me and he says that."

"I'm sorry to hear that."

"And he makes fun of my name. Says my mother insisted on it, out of some book she read, but he thinks it's a pansy name. He says terrible things. He says my mother spent too much time in church. Says all that time in church never helped her beat the cancer. I'm goin' to live out on the road. I'm not goin' back to Decatur."

"I know you're not. That's an awful thing to say."

"It's bad to get walloped, too, but now I'm wonderin' if maybe I oughta give it a try, diggin' ditches."

"Was he drinkin' when he said those things? Well? Sidney, you said you'd tell me the truth."

"Sometimes he does tip the bottle, I can't lie about it."

The boxcar fell silent, and the tracks played their low, clicking music. The old man wheezed and said, "Now Sidney, I have to tell you somethin' important. When a man gets bit by the drinkin' bug, it's like he becomes somebody else, somebody he shouldn't be. Maybe you're askin' how I know about it. Well, it's because I used to be like that. I used to be bitten by the drinkin' bug. So I do know. It won't be easy to do, and maybe it's not fair for me to ask you to do it, but I want you to do somethin' for me: Those mean things your dad did and said when he was drinkin'—I'm guessin' there was a lot more of them. Well, I need you to start thinkin' like he wasn't the one who did and said them."

"What? But he walloped me and he said those things, Pat—over and over."

"I know it seems like he did, but the truth is somebody else took over."

"You're crazy. That was my dad."

"No."

"Who then?"

"Somebody not very nice. That wasn't your dad who said that to you about the ditches. That was this other fella."

"Who?"

"The mean fella. The guy who comes on duty because your dad got bit by the bug."

Sidney stared at his companion.

"That's his job, you see, Sidney. To say terrible things. Do terrible things. But he's not your dad, that mean fella. He works for the shadows. He likes to take men over."

The boy considered this.

"How do you know about all this?"

"I've met this fella. I know what he does. I know how he works."

A long silence followed, and it looked to Pat like Sidney was looking for something through the wide gap in the boxcar door.

"I miss my mom," Sidney said. "He never drank at all before my mom died. I miss her all the time."

"I bet you do, Sidney."

"My dad never walloped me before she passed."

"That's the way it is when a man gets bit by the bug. It's like I say: Someone else comes right into your body, someone bad, when you're most vulnerable. It happened to me. I bet if you try, you can remember a lotta good things about your dad—your real dad, not the mean fella. Wasn't he kinder to you when your mom was around? And wouldn't she want you to remember that, too?"

Sidney made no answer. Pat rasped out a long cough over the clicking of the train car. Then he said, "I believe your dad was attacked, Sidney. That's the truth. That's what happened. Satan can attack a man and take him over and make a demon keep him company, unless Christ strengthens the man."

Sidney kept looking through the boxcar door.

"Even if I do start thinkin' like you say," Sidney said, "I ain't goin' back to Decatur."

"I know you ain't, Sidney. I know."

"Pat, can I ask you somethin'?"

"Sure."

"How long is it since you had a drink?"

"Four years, seven months, three days."

"You ever wanna drink anymore?"

"Sure."

"You ever buy liquor anymore, or ask anybody to give it to you?"

"Not yet. Jesus help me, I don't ever wanna do either of those things again. That's the truth, Sidney. My prayer is, 'I can do all things through Christ, who strengthens me.'"

"You think my dad could stop drinkin' if he wanted to? If he said that prayer, I mean?"

"Oh I'm sure he could, Sidney."

The iron wheels clacked for a good long time.

Then the boy said, "I thought about askin' somebody to buy me some liquor tonight."

"I pray to God you don't ever do that, Sidney. Now I need you to think of your dad as someone who got bit by a bug. Like he caught the Spanish flu. Or the polio. You wouldn't get mad at someone who caught the polio, would you?"

"Don't wanna say."

"Could you try, Sidney? Could you try to think of him that way? Just for one minute?"

"Maybe."

"Can you imagine him regrettin' what he said and did to hurt you?"

"I guess. If he were sick. Like you said."

"Well, can't you try to forgive him for lettin' that other fella take over while he was sick? The mean fella? I swear he doesn't want that mean fella around. He just can't help it now. Once you make the mistake of lettin' that fella in, he's awfully hard to get rid of. Will you try to forgive your father, Sidney?"

"I'll think about it."

"It doesn't mean forgettin' about anything he did. It doesn't mean you approve of anything he did either. It just means you don't live your life mad at that other guy. The shadow guy. Otherwise, he'll take you over too, you see."

Sidney thought about these things through a long stretch of central Illinois. It was dark in the boxcar, and it was hard to see unless there was a light outside flickering past. Every once in a while, he could sneak a look at Pat as a streetlight sent a broad arc of light through the boxcar door. He wanted to see if the old guy still looked alive. He did, but not by much.

Some time later, without warning, Pat threw a leather pouch, tied at the top with a tiny red strap, toward Sidney's corner of the boxcar. Then Pat said, "Sidney, I've got twenty-four dollars and eleven cents saved up in that pouch. I'd like you to think about getting off at Centralia and holdin' on to that money until we see each other again. Spend it if you hit an emergency, though. Fair enough?"

He gave another racking cough. Sidney studied him for a

long moment, picked up the pouch, untied the red strap, and looked inside. He set the pouch down and asked, "Did you ever do somethin' very bad? Maybe somethin' you're tryin' to make up for?"

"If I did, that's between me and my God."

"Pat, are you goin' to die tonight?"

"I already answered that one for you, Sidney. It doesn't make any sense at all to ask me the same question over and over again."

"Well, why do you want me to take your money?"

"It's just a precaution. Only spend it if you have to. If there's an emergency, say. I'm just askin' you to hold onto it until we see each other again."

"And when's that likely to be?"

"We're the dukes of the rails, Sidney. We never know the answer to that. But I know we're goin' to see each other again. I have a good feelin' about that."

Sidney took the pouch and put it in his pocket.

"Thank you," said Pat. "Will you do somethin' else for me, Sidney?"

"What's that?"

"Will you say my prayer out loud?"

"I don't remember it."

"I can say it for you again if you want. You're goin' to have some hard times once you get off. I don't want that mean guy gettin' to you, you see. And I don't think your mom does, either."

"Go ahead and say it, then."

Pat mouthed the words with some effort: "I can do all things through Christ, who strengthens me."

"I can do all things through Christ, who strengthens me," Sidney repeated.

"Do you accept Jesus as your Savior, Sidney?"

Sidney sniffed and looked out the open boxcar door and then said:

"Yes, I do."

"Hallelujah!" the older man cried. "Hallelujah! Now when you get to Centralia, you're goin' to look for a hotel called the Apollo. You can check your suitcase there for just a quarter a week. Don't spend any money on a room. You can't afford that now. You just ask that hotel clerk to point you toward a man called Desmond Rider, and you tell him that Pat Walsh said you should seek him out. The clerk will know who Desmond is. Desmond stays there all the time. When you see Desmond, tell him you talked to me and that I can vouch for you as a hard worker at harvest time. You're goin' to be a hard worker at harvest time, aren't you, Sidney?"

"Yes, I will. I swear it."

"All right, then. You may sleep in a couple of haystacks, and you may have to follow the crops around for a while, and you may have to jump a couple of boxcars to do it, but as long as you stay in touch with Desmond, you'll be all right. He's in Centralia for at least another three weeks. He can point you to where the work is, and he'll make sure you get paid. You got all that?"

"Yes, Pat."

"You don't mind sleepin' outside until you have a little more money saved up?"

"No, Pat. I don't mind."

"Good. Centralia's the next stop. You've got about two minutes, I guess. You'd better get yourself ready. Now no more ridin' the rails at midnight, Sidney. You're too young for that. That's an order. If you'd stayed on this car to the end of the line, I know you would've regretted it—and I would've, too. There's always some bad characters waitin' for a young man without family at the end of this line."

"Pat, are you goin' to be all right?"

"Course I am, Sidney, course I am. Don't worry. We'll see each other again."

He let out another low, grievous cough, and it didn't end until the train began to slow and Sidney could see the Centralia station approaching through the open boxcar door.

Pat pointed at the station and said "Go" like he meant it, so Sidney stood, walked over to the old man in the corner who had saved his soul, shook his cold hand, kissed him on the forehead like he was kin, and hopped off the boxcar.

The old man smiled the broadest smile of his life when the train pulled out of Centralia, and that smile was still on his face when they found him at the end of the line. It was a smile of gratitude.

"Your faith can move mountains and your doubt can create them."

—ANONYMOUS

TAKING
STOCK

Each moment you breathe is a gift.

—OPRAH WINFREY

The book you are holding in your hands has been a labor of love for me. It is the culmination of many encounters, experiences, mistakes made, fences mended, and lessons learned—not always easily or quickly—over a long span of years. In these pages, I have sometimes used dramatic license to illustrate the importance, the validity, and the enduring relevance of life lessons that have gotten me through hard times, lessons that might not have registered as strongly or as memorably otherwise. To close the book, I want to share a story that is completely true.

Recently I came across a little blue book with an extended handwritten entry. My father, John Klobucher, wrote that entry in 1938, a number of years before I was born. It begins:

In about 1800, in village Knezina, County Crnomelj (Austria at that time) was Family Brickole, whose girl took for her mate Klobucar from neighboring village. Son Stefan was born about 1805. About 1830, Stefan's first daughter, Kate, was born. Died 1906. She was the oldest daughter of my grandfather, whose name also was Stefan. Grandfather married about 1865. Son Stefan III was born 1868, died 1934.

The text goes on at length, briskly noting everything about our family's genealogy that my father knew from personal experience or had been able to dig up through his own research, as well as all the major events from his own life, some of which—including the difficult trip to America and its aftermath, the dangerous stint in the copper mine, and the long-distance courtship—I've fictionalized here. He'd spent quite a lot of time thinking about who he was and where he came from, and he obviously wanted

156

to make sure he recorded everything properly. His handwritten entry concludes as follows:

September 13, 1938. Today (my birthday) I am writing after visiting Knezina, Dragatus, and Llublajana in Yugoslavia. The above are nearest to my birthplace in Europe. It's wise to take inventory. See what you are, who you are, but do not hold it against yourself nor pride yourself too much. We are just men, not more not less. What others make for us is not real, not dependable, and often harmful. Do it for yourself.

I encountered these wise and uniquely memorable words for the first time during the year I was working on this book. They had a galvanizing effect on me. What I believe my father was saying—to me and to the world—was that we are each responsible for understanding our own life story. Not only that: We are each responsible for deriving our own *meaning and purpose* from that story. That's what I've tried to do here.

These stories are my own way of taking inventory, as my father took stock of his life to that point eight decades ago. The transformational tales between these covers have come to mean a lot to me. I hope they mean something to you, too, and I hope they inspire you to take advantage of the opportunity to take your own inventory, to see what you are and who you are, and to create some stories of your own ... and to be grateful!

Epilogue

Thanks for reading this, my first book of short stories. Before we say goodbye, let me share what I believe are some very wise words on gratitude as this book's final, transformational lesson:

"Give thanks to the God of heaven. His love endures forever." (Psalm 136:26)

For many centuries, this verse has reminded people of many nations, races, and backgrounds of a powerful, abiding truth about the human experience, namely: No matter what is taking place in your life right now, and no matter how you may feel about what's happening, you can always find something to be grateful for. If you choose, you can embrace gratitude. I believe that if you're truly a believing person, you *must* make the effort to live as much of your life as possible in that state of thankfulness, and I believe that, once you make up your mind to do so, you will be a better, happier person.

This is the great lesson of my own life. Gratitude has been a transformative force for me in each phase of my own personal growth and development. Every time I've made the choice to let gratitude into my world, it's changed my world for the better. And not only that—I've noticed that, once I do find something in my experience to be authentically grateful for, it's literally impossible for me to hold onto a negative thought pattern. Perhaps you'll find the same to be true in your life.

Let me close by saying that I am grateful for all the miles traveled in a long life, all the lessons learned, and all the good people I've met along the way. I am grateful for having had the opportunity to complete this project, and grateful that you, the reader, made it this far in the book with me.

And most of all, I am grateful to God for his unending love.

—TOM KLOBUCHER

OTHER BOOKS BY TOM KLOBUCHER

The Great Workplace Revolution takes the reader through the twelve essential strategies for creating a great place to work—and provides the tools to better understand and leverage the unique giftedness of the five distinct workplace generations that will be working together in this most exciting decade!

The Great Workplace Transformation is a learning parable that shows business leaders how to hire and retain the most creative, loyal, and growth-driven employees, transforming their workplaces into powerhouses that thrive in the present multi-generational environment!

The Tailor's Son is an authentic American story on classic themes: Father, son, and the healing power of belief. Here Tom takes a loving look back at the perils of youth, the distance that can arise between father and son, and the potential for reconciliation and positive change.

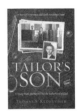

Retirement: The Best Is Yet to Come provides the retirement roadmap for the time of your life! What is the secret to a successful retirement? Tom shares twenty-five bold steps to a happy, positive, fulfilled and engaged retirement!

Transformational Relationships is a learning tool for every generation that traces our positive transformational relationships—from early childhood to our senior years—and prepares us for our very best life!

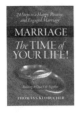

Marriage: The Time of Your Life helps readers discover the great treasure of an engaged, transformational marriage—and to live happily ever after!

WANT TO LEARN MORE?

Please join us at www.amazon.com/author/thomasklobucher
or www.talkswithtom.com

Tom Klobucher, Founder, CEO, Author & Speaker

Thomas Interiors, Inc.

476 Brighton Drive

Bloomingdale, IL 60108

630 980 4200

tomk@thomasinteriors.com